HALLOWEEN FLIGHT 77

By

Debbie Madison

ISBN: 0-75965-652-5

This book is printed on acid free paper.

1stBooks – rev. 8/20/01

CHAPTER 1

"I'm coming, I'm coming!" I yelled as I dashed toward the kitchen phone. I grabbed the receiver with my right hand as I glanced at my watch. Damn, I thought I'm already late. "Yes, I mean hello," I said as I slipped my feet into my nursing shoes. "Hello?" I repeated in haste.

"Oh," the soft voice replied, "hello I didn't think anyone was home, is this Mrs. Thompson?"

"Yes, I'm Mrs. Thompson and I'm late for work. Who is this? What do you want?" The tone in my voice and my blunt questions must have surprised the caller for she hesitated a few seconds before she replied.

"Mrs. Thompson," she said, "please pick up your son Jeremy. He was caught smoking on campus again and has been suspended from school."

The caller's tiny sweet voice didn't impress me. "What? Smoking again? Are you sure? Who is this?" I bombarded it with questions.

"I'm Mrs. Motto," she replied, "Mr. Terrace, the principal's secretary. He wants me to make an appointment with you and your husband to see him about your son as soon as possible. What day would be good for you?"

I hesitated a few seconds then exploded, "Jeremy's not my son and I really don't care what you do with him, screw him! I'm not going to be late for work ever again because of him. As far as I'm concerned he can stay at school till he rots!"

I slammed the receiver down my hands were shaking. I grabbed my purse and headed outside. I could hear the phone ringing as I ran out the back door and into the driveway. What had I just done?

I yanked my car into gear and floored it, work was only ten minutes away. If I was lucky and hit every green light I could make it in about five. I couldn't be late for work today, I just couldn't.

Jeremy had gotten into a fight on Monday and I was two hours late then, today was only Wednesday. My boss was very understanding but on Monday afternoon she made it quite clear to me that if I was late once again this week I would be fired.

This was the best job I've ever had I couldn't loose it. Why? Why? was my stepson doing this to me? Why couldn't he behave like my daughter Katie? She always did her homework on time and never complained or caused me any problems.

I took a deep breath as I plowed through the signal lights. Come on, come on, turn green.

My heart raced as I dodged in and out of traffic. I recklessly floored it through a yellow light and slammed my brakes on as the car in front of me abruptly changed lanes.

What am I doing? I thought as my seat belt dug into my chest. I'm going to get killed driving like this. I glanced at my watch, it was 9:05am I was already late. My heart sank as I pulled into the hospitals parking lot. Should I go upstairs and face my boss? Or should I just turn around and pick up Jeremy? Either way I would get yelled at.

I pushed my station wagons gear into park as I grabbed my nursing hat and stethoscope and hurried upstairs.

I purposely avoided the elevator. Janet, my boss was always close by it watching for employees who showed up late.

Some how she always managed to keep a smile on her face but when she talked directly to you, you could tell by the look in her eyes that she meant business.

Over the past six months Janet had taken me in under her wings. She knew how badly my x-husband had treated me. She knew this job was my new beginning and how much it had turned my life around.

Please God, I prayed let Janet be out on a break.

Three flights of stairs left me gasping for air as I cautiously opened the stairwell door. Janet was nowhere in sight. I poked my head further inside looking up and down the hallways, the coast was clear. I hurried through the door and made a beeline to the nursing station.

"You're late!" Rhonda said as she hung up the telephone and turned toward me. "What's your excuse today?"

"Sh...Sh... Please don't tell Janet." I begged as I put my purse down. "Please Rhonda, I really need this job."

"Relax," Rhonda said as she smiled while picking up my time card, "I clocked you in early today."

Sprinting up three flights of stairs had left me short of breath. I composed myself while reading the patient's charts as I walked into the first room.

"Good morning Timmy," I pulled my eyes away from his chart look directly at him and cheerfully asked, "How are you feeling today?"

Timmy immediately turned his head away from me and buried it deeper into his pillow. This frightened little boy was only eight years old and was recovering from a horrible car crash that had broken both of his legs. From his hips down he was entombed in a thick white cast.

His room was filled with balloons and stuffed animals. He had an iron grip on a small brown teddy bear that was peaking out of his blanket. Both of his parents had been badly injured in the same crash and weren't well enough to talk or visit him despite being right here in the same hospital.

I felt so sorry for him, every free minute I had, I read him stories. He had been in here for almost a week and hadn't spoken a word to anyone. Whenever I showed him pictures from storybooks he would turn his head away from me. I knew he must of felt awfully frightened and alone.

"Are you ready for another story Timmy?" I asked as I opened a book and sat down on the bed next to him.

"I want my mom, do you know where she is? I want to go home." Timmy's face was still buried in his pillow as he spoke. Tears ran down his cheeks, he tried to hide them. I couldn't imagine being eight years old and all alone. I put the book down and turned his small head towards me.

"I didn't know you could talk Timmy, everyone here at the hospital thinks that you don't know how to speak, this is wonderful." I stroked his thick blond hair and said, "I've got an idea, lets get you a wheelchair and we'll go find your parents, okay?"

Timmy's eyes opened wide while he looked at me. "Do you mean it?" he asked, "Do you really mean it?"

The sad tone in his voice convinced me that I had to at least, try. "I promise," I replied, "But, first I have to get permission and I have to find out where your parents are." I squeezed his small hands and smiled at him as I stood up from his bed. His eyes followed me as I left the room.

As I put Timmy's chart away my boss Janet walked up to Rhonda and started talking to her. Rhonda's facial expressions painted an ugly picture as Janet spoke. I didn't need to hear the conversation I knew something was wrong.

Rhonda glanced at me then back at Janet. I could see tears swelling in her eyes. I grabbed Timmy's chart and hastened my pace back to his room.

Janet stopped me at his door, "And how are you doing today Mary?" She asked as she held her hand out for Timmy's chart.

"Just fine," I replied as I forced a nervous smile to my face. "And how is little Timmy feeling today?" She asked as she fingered through his chart.

"He's better," I replied, "But he's really lonely. Janet can I take him in a wheel chair to see his parents? Please. And guess what?" I added, "He actually talked to me this morning."

Janet pulled her face out of his chart for a moment and stared deeply into my eyes.

"I'm not sure," she said, "Check with the charge nurse on the fifth floor. See how Timmy's parents are feeling. If it's all right with her, then it's fine with me."

Janet closed the chart and took a step closer towards me. It made me uncomfortable. She hesitated a few seconds then asked, "Mary, were you late today?"

She calmly stood directly in front of me pumpkin smile and all, waiting for a reply.

My first response was to say no, for I really needed this job. Be honest, tell her the truth a little voice in side of me kept repeating, I bit my lower lip and replied, "Yes Janet, I was late today. My stepson got in trouble at school again this morning."

3

Janet's facial expressions rarely changed, they made me nervous. "Did you ask Rhonda to clock you in this morning?" She asked without blinking an eye.

"No," I replied without hesitation, "I would never cheat." I was tongue-tied, I didn't want to get Rhonda in trouble but I also couldn't lie. "No," I repeated, "I didn't" I felt terrible and hung my head down in shame.

"I see," Janet said as she handed me Timmy's chart back. "I'm glad to hear that Timmy's talking and doing so well," she added as she walked away.

I waited till she turned the hall corner then I walked over to where Rhonda was sitting. Guilt was written all over her face. Her eyes were puffy and red.

"I'm sorry," I said, "I didn't mean to get you in trouble." I felt awful, Rhonda had saved my job this morning and now I had gotten her in trouble. "I'm so sorry," I repeated.

"It's not your fault Mary," Rhonda said as she blew her nose into a Kleenex then confessed, "I've been clocking everyone on this floor in on time for months. I just get up early and figured everyone here would like me if I clocked them in early."

"Are you fired?" I boldly asked. "Yes," Rhonda sobbed as she blew her nose again.

"Don't worry about it," I said as I looked up and glanced around the room. "I'm fired too. We can go to the unemployment office together, ok?"

Rhonda looked up towards my face as I looked down at hers, our eyes met. For some silly reason we both started laughing. She stood up and we hugged each other.

Timmy's room buzzer beeped, our front office phone started ringing at the same time.

"I got the phone," Rhonda said as she blew her nose again and grabbed another piece of Kleenex.

"Okay" I replied, "I'll check on Timmy." As I headed towards his room I started thinking about what Janet had said to me. I couldn't remember if she had told me I was fired or not. How stupid can I be, I thought. I don't even remember if my boss just fired me. I remember her telling me on Monday that if I was late one more day this week, I would be fired. But today after I admitted being late Janet didn't say I was fired, or had she?

It was barely ten in the morning and I was already exhausted and a nervous wreck. Somehow in the last two hours I had managed to alienate my stepson, his principal, probably my wonderful new husband and somehow I had just got both my friend Rhonda and myself fired.

Timmy's eyes were still waiting at the door for me as I entered his room, what a wonderful sight. He wasn't hiding under his pillow or covers. Seeing the sadness lifted from his long thin face made me feel good all over. I sat down on his bed next to him and put all my worries behind me.

"How come you didn't come back?" He asked as he studied my face.

"I'm sorry," I said, "We're very busy today but I haven't forgotten about you. My boss Janet just told me that if your parents are well enough, I could take you to visit them.

"What does that mean?" Timmy's smile faded and a frown filled his face. "How come I can't see them? Don't they want to see me?"

Timmy was a pleasure to be around. I enjoyed his simple questions. Right now I wished I could join him and become a child again so my life wouldn't be so complex.

"Lets get you up and see how you feel," I said as I rolled a specially designed wheel chair into the room. "If you can sit comfortably in this wheel chair, then I'll let you be my assistant all day today, okay?"

"What about my parents," Timmy wasn't going to let me change the subject, he crossed his arms together and said, "I want to see them, you promised me you would take me to see my parents."

Timmy was right I had promised him. Without thinking what was right or wrong or getting permission from anyone I quickly and carefully lifted Timmy out of bed and onto a specially designed wheel chair.

He was bottom heavy and lifting him tweaked the lower muscles in my back. The pain didn't bother me, I wanted to make this little boy happy.

I figured I was already fired and if I waited for permission from all the people I should have, it could have taken hours.

Timmy had confided in me and I wasn't about to lose his trust. His eyes lit up as I slowly spinned him in a circle making sure he was locked safely and comfortably in the wheel chair.

"Again," He kept repeating as we spinned, first left then back around to the right.

Rhonda walked into the room with a puzzled look on her face, "Mary, what are you doing? Timmy's not suppose to be out of bed. What are you doing?"

"I'm taking Timmy upstairs to see his parents" I replied. "Rhonda, please don't try and stop me. He needs to see his parents."

"No!" Rhonda raised her voice and said, "No Mary! I won't let you take Timmy out of this room. You will get in trouble."

"Trouble" I laughed, "Somehow in the last three hours I've managed to alienate my husband, my stepson, his principal and I've been fired! I don't think I can get in any more trouble today, however Rhonda I could use some help. Would you like to get fired again today?" I teased.

The puzzled look on face quickly faded. She smiled at me and said, "Sure, why not."

"Thanks Rhonda, I need you to find out Timmy's parents room numbers and tell his parents to shoo away the nurses from their rooms because we are on our way up to visit them right now."

"Yippee!" Timmy shouted, "Lets go."

His enthusiasm sparked Rhonda and I into first gear. "I'll meet you at the elevator" "and" I continued, "Rhonda be careful watch out for Janet."

"Lets go! Vroom, Vroom," Timmy started flapping his arms around pretending his wheel chair was a racecar.

"Shhhh..Timmy, you have to be quiet, do you understand?" Timmy ignored what I said and kept shouting, "Lets Go!"

"Quiet, shhhh.." I closed his room door so no one else could hear us. "Timmy," I said, "If you're not quiet we can't go find your parents. It's very important that you remain quiet. Can you be quiet? I asked. Not just a little bit quiet I mean real, real quiet. Like when you first came here to the hospital, real quiet."

I was standing in front of Timmy's wheel chair looking directly at him. The glow on his face alone was enough to keep me from changing my mind I was ready.

Timmy was ready. He responded by immediately becoming quiet. I threw a blanket over his head, covering most of his face.

"I will go slow," I whispered, "Please keep quiet."

His room door opened sending my heart pounding. It was Rhonda. "You scared me." I said as I tightened my handgrip on Timmy's wheel chair.

"My husbands not going to believe this one," Rhonda joked as she inched her head out Timmy's door looking up and down the halls. "All clear," She announced, "Go now."

I didn't hesitate I rolled Timmy out of his room, then quickly down the hall towards the back elevators.

"Room 518 and ICU," Rhonda shouted as the elevator dinged for us to come aboard.

"ICU," I shouted back, "Are you sure?"

"Yes," I heard Rhonda say as the elevator doors closed in front of us.

"What is ICU?" Timmy asked. "Is that good?"

All my plans suddenly seemed wrong. I couldn't take Timmy to ICU. That was the Intensive Care Unit. It was for patients that were really sick or dying. Oh my God, I thought what if his parents are dying?

My heart sank, what am I doing? I thought. Why didn't I listen to Janet? My stomach turned.

The intensive care unit was for people in a comma and hanging on to life by sometimes, just a thread. Most of the patients there had tubes in their arms, legs, nose and sometimes their heads. Should I expose an eight year old to this? Wouldn't it be better if Timmy remembered his parents the way they were before this accident?

The elevator door chimed bringing my thoughts back to earth before it was too late. We were already at the fifth floor. I pushed back my fears and concerns as the elevator door opened.

I composed myself and headed down the hall. I turned my head away from the doctors and nurses as I passed them. I was very nervous, thank god no one questioned me. Why should they? I was a nurse pushing a wheel chair.

Timmy was wonderful he remained silent and never made a noise until we entered his mother's room.

"Mom!" he suddenly yelled, "Mom!" His skinny arms stretched out as he reached for her bed, "Are you all right? How come you haven't come to my room"?

His warmth and affection brought tears to my eyes. His mother's face was badly bruised and swollen. She had extensive stitches above her left eye that ran all the way up her face past her ear. One of her arms was in a thick white cast. Her eyes were buried in deep dark circles and they looked hollow even though they were partially opened.

"Timmy," she murmured, "Thank god you're alive." Her voice was barely discernable but Timmy heard her.

A tear ran down her cheek, her lips were quivering as she spoke.

"Your son is doing very well," I whispered as I moved Timmy closer. Both of his legs are broken but they are mending fast.

Timmy latched onto his mother's hand and held on to it tightly with both of his hands. "They wouldn't let me see you mom, I thought you were dead. Can I stay in here with you?"

I could see the pain on Timmy's mother's face as she struggled to speak.

"Timmy," I quickly interrupted, "Your mother needs a lot of rest. If you stay with her, she will want to stay awake and keep you company. Right now she needs to sleep."

Timmy's mother's face muscles twitched bringing a smile to her battered face. A second later it disappeared she closed her eyes.

"Is my mom all right?" Timmy asked as he tapped on her arm trying to get her to open her eyes again.

"Mom, can you hear me? Please open your eyes. Mary," Timmy asked, "how come my mom won't talk to me? Are you sure she is still alive?"

Timmy's smile faded from his face almost as fast as his mother's had.

"Is my mom going to die?" he asked with a sad look on his face as he rubbed his hands up and down her arm.

"No Timmy," I replied without thinking, "I won't let her die, I promise you she will be all right. Right now what your mom needs is to rest and sleep for a long time."

"How long?" Timmy asked as he turned his head around and looked up at me. "How long does my mom have to sleep?"

"I don't know," I replied, "But I'll check on her every day and I'll let her know how you are doing."

Her room door opened with a loud squeak. It surprised me and shot adrenaline to every inch of my body.

A short heavyset woman entered the room. "Who are you?" she asked, "What are you doing here?" She eased her way over to the security alarm button.

"Wait!" I shouted, "Its ok, I work here." I pointed to the security badge attached to my uniform. "This is Timmy's mother."

"Whose mother?" The nurse kept a safe distance from me as she looked around the room.

"My mom," Timmy replied. "This is my mom."

"Why aren't you in the pediatric ward? Who gave you permission to come upstairs?" What did you say your name was?"

"Look lady," I hastily said, "We aren't strangers. Timmy missed his mother so I brought him upstairs to see her it's that simple. Wouldn't you do the same for your own child?"

The surprised look on the nurse's face faded but she was still inching closer to the alarm button.

"I'm sorry," I said, "I'll take Timmy back to his room right now. Please don't call security."

"No!" Timmy yelled, "I'm staying right here with my mom I'm not leaving this room."

Before Timmy could throw a tantrum or the nurse could press the security alarm I twirled his wheel chair around and pushed it out the door.

"Calm down," I whispered closely to his ear. "Stop yelling, if you don't I won't be allowed to take you to see your father. Do you understand me Timmy?"

I lifted my head up and glanced around the room. The nurse was standing in the doorway of his mother's room her eyes followed us as we got on the elevator. We both waved at her hoping she wouldn't call security.

"Where is my dad?" Timmy asked as the elevator door closed. "Is he as sick as my mom?"

"He's down on the first floor," I replied, "but I don't know if I should take you there Timmy."

"What do you mean?" Timmy twisted his head around and looked up at me. "Why not? Is my dad dying?"

I took a deep breath and replied, "Timmy I'll be honest with you. I don't have time to find out how your father is doing. He might look pretty bad right now. I mean," I hesitated for a few moments gathering my thoughts. I didn't know how to explain the intensive care unit to and eight year old child.

"Timmy, I don't want you to remember your father like this."

"Like what? He asked, "Please, please take me to see my dad." Tears swelled in his eyes. He turned away from me to hide them, "please" He repeated, "Take me see my dad. I miss him and I really want to talk to him."

Our elevator stopped at the second floor. Oh no I though, it's all over now, the door opened, my heart skipped a beat.

"There you are," Rhonda's voice flooded the elevator as she stepped inside and quickly pushed the close button behind her.

She stood directly in front of us blocking our view from everyone.

"Shh, shh," She whispered, "Be very quiet," As the door closed she burst into conversation.

"Your husband has called, the school has called and the nurse from the fifth floor has called. Security is looking for you. Where are you going, Mary?"

I needed a minute to think. I pushed the stop button. The elevator came to an abrupt halt. "We need a plan," I said. "Rhonda, I promised Timmy I would take him to see his father and that's exactly what I am going to do."

Rhonda shook her head in disagreement, "I think you're nuts Mary, oh all right I'll help you. I guess I didn't want to collect unemployment after all."

Once again Rhonda's and my eyes met. This time there was no laughter between us. A deep silence crept around the elevator.

"What's the plan?" Timmy asked. "Why do we need a plan? What does a plan mean?"

I didn't pay any attention to Timmy. I had to concentrate on the thoughts at hand.

"I've got it!" I said. I whispered in Rhonda's ear until the elevator door chimed.

Rhonda and I shared a nervous glance then we left the elevator in opposite directions. She headed down the hall towards the intensive care unit. Timmy and I headed up the hall towards the closest bathroom. Luckily for us it was within eyesight.

I quickly moved the wheel chair inside and locked the door behind me. I knew security would be looking for the two of us and I figured I would have a better chance finding Timmy's father by myself.

"Okay," I whispered to Timmy, "the coast is clear. You stay inside this bathroom until I come back and get you. Keep the door locked and be real quiet. I promise, I will be back in just a few minutes."

Timmy opened his mouth to talk, I knew he had a lot of questions. I put my hand over his mouth. "Shh.. shh.. You have to trust me," I said, "You have to be real quiet while I find your dad. I will knock three times to let you know it's me. Don't answer the door until you hear three knocks, do you understand?"

Timmy's smile faded and turned into a frustrated stare as he watched me leave the room.

I knew he was tired and I knew he was becoming very impatient. All he wanted to do was see his father I bent over and hugged him.

"I promise," I added, "I will be right back."

I peaked out the bathroom door and waited till the coast was clear. The ICU beds were only a few feet away from me. I could hear people talking but I couldn't see them. Their voices were calm, I assumed no one had found out about us yet.

Rhonda had worked ICU two years ago. Somehow she was going to distract the nurses while I slipped Timmy's wheel chair by them.

As I tip toed down the hallway a loud deafening noise filled the room. It startled me I ran back and hid in the bathroom with Timmy.

"Wow! That was fast," Timmy said, "What's that noise?"

"I think it's our cue," I said as I grabbed on tight to the wheel chair and pushed Timmy out into the hall.

The hall was empty I didn't hesitate. I pushed the wheelchair as fast as I could toward the ICU beds. I could see the nurse's station it was directly in front of us. My heart jumped into my throat. I tried to stay calm as I cautiously walked by the nurse's station.

"Dad! That's my dad!" Timmy yelled. "Quiet!" I shouted.

It was too late, a tall slender man appeared from behind the counter. He didn't try to stop me as we entered Timmy's father's room he just picked up the phone.

"Dad, Dad!" Timmy cried as he tried to jump out of his wheelchair. "Are you ok?"

I glanced at Timmy's father then back outside the room. The tall nurse was still on the phone and had been joined by two other women in nursing uniforms. All three of them were pointing and staring at us.

Timmy was talking to his father and holding his hand. His dad was motionless. "What's wrong with you?" Timmy cried, "Dad can you hear me? Please talk to me?'

Tears swelled in my eyes as Timmy spilled his heart out to his Father. I grabbed his father's chart and glanced through it.

His father had a concussion, a punctured lung and three broken ribs. He was unconscious and hadn't regained consciousness since the accident almost a week ago.

His vitals were stable and now all anyone could do was wait and hope that he would regain consciousness.

Oh my God, I thought how do I explain this to Timmy. I looked up from the chart as two security guards opened our room door.

"Everything is going to be alright Mary," One of the guards said, "Just relax, we're not going to hurt you." Adrenalin shot through me, my heart screamed. I don't know why but I wasn't afraid, I felt strong. I felt like I could run past both of them if I wanted to. I blinked my eyes repeatedly as I tried to figure out what to do.

"Leave the boy alone," I said in a deep authoritative voice as I turned toward the guards and put my hands in the air. "I will come with you if you leave Timmy alone."

Both guards slowly inched into the room circling on opposite sides around me.

"Stop!" I screamed, "I won't leave unless you promise the boy can stay with his father." I grabbed a syringe from the supply shelf behind me. "I mean it!" I screamed, "Back up! I want your promise that Timmy can stay with his father."

The guards glanced back and forth at each other as I threatened them, by stabbing the needle towards them.

"We don't want to hurt you," one of them said, "and we know you don't want to hurt Timmy."

"Please. Please," I cried, "Just promise me Timmy can stay here with his father, that's all I'm asking!"

I fought back tears as I spoke. Everything around me seemed to be moving in slow motion.

"Dad!" Timmy yelled again, "Wake up! Please wake up." Timmy was crying and started screaming.

Tears flooded my face as my hands and entire body began to shake.

"Now!" one guard yelled. I turned towards him and stabbed the syringe at him. He backed up as the other guard slammed into my back so forcefully that it knocked the needle out of my hand and sent me flying across the room as me knees buckled from under me.

My body slammed onto the hard linoleum floor. I grabbed for the needle. The guard latched onto my arm and quickly whipped it behind my back. The other guard grabbed my left arm and tightly twisted it into my back.

Pain shot up my spine. "We got her!" they both yelled.

"No!" Timmy screamed. "Leave her alone, she's my friend, stop it! Dad, please help me. Wake up."

I looked up from the floor at Timmy. A woman was wheeling him out of the room. He was waving his arms lashing out at her. "No, leave me here. Dad, please stop them."

"Wait!" A voice shouted over all of the commotion. "Stop, leave the boy alone. Look! Look!"

My ears followed the voice to a familiar face. It was my boss, Janet. She was standing in the doorway pointing towards the bed. "Look, it's Mr. Richfield, he's moving."

"Dad! Timmy screamed," "Don't let them take me away."

The guards pulled me up from the ground to my feet. "Let her go!" Janet's voice shook the room with a tone in it I hadn't heard before she wasn't smiling. She walked over and stood directly in front of the guards.

"You heard me, I said let her go. This isn't a police station this is a hospital. What in God's name are you doing to my nurse?"

The stern tone in her voice was persuasive. Both guards immediately released the death grip from my arms and unlocked the handcuffs.

"She threatened us with a syringe, she's dangerous." Both guards spoke out defending their actions.

"Get out of here! Both of you," Janet glanced at Mr. Richfield's bed then back towards the guards. "Right now!"

"Mary," She continued, "Get that boy back in here. Can't you see his father is waking up."

I heard Janet but my body was still in shock, I couldn't move. Janet turned around once again looking back at me. "Mary," She said in a much softer voice, "Timmy wants to see his father. Please wheel him back into the room." The pumpkin smile she always wore returned to her face.

This time I didn't hesitate, "Yes Mam," I held my breath then walked out the door towards the wheel chair. Every inch of my body was shaking, I tried not to show it.

"Is my dad finally awake?" Timmy stretched his neck past me trying to see his dad's bed. "I'm out here dad," he shouted, "Can you see me?"

I quickly wheeled him back inside the room and parked his wheelchair right next to his father's pillow.

Two nurses entered the room. One walked around checking all the electronic equipment scattered throughout the room. The other one started talking to Mr. Richfield. His eyes remained closed but his arms were moving.

"Timmy," I said, "talk to your dad, let him know that you are here."

Timmy grabbed his father's left hand. "Dad," He kept repeating, "It's me Timmy please wake up, can you hear me?"

Janet was standing behind me only a few feet away the room was crowded.

As Timmy talked to his father an unexplainable warmth filled the room. It blanketed my quivering body. I took a deep breath almost a sigh of relief as I glanced around the room.

Rhonda had joined us, she was standing in the doorway. Without saying a word she waved goodbye and left.

I wasn't sure if what I had just done was right, but I felt good about it. As Timmy talked to his father my thoughts drifted.

Puzzling questions kept entering my mind. Why did my boss Janet protect me? Why wasn't I arrested? Why was she still standing directly behind me?

"Look!" Timmy yelled, "My dad is opening his eyes! I think he can hear me, I think he is going to be okay." "Dad," he said in a much quieter voice, "It's me Timmy, can you see me?"

Mr. Richfield's eyes opened. They slowly blinked, over and over again. The rest of his face remained motionless.

"Dad," Timmy said, "What's wrong? Can't you see me?'

"Mary," Timmy cried, "Can't my dad see me?" I didn't know what to say to Timmy. I looked up and around the room searching for an answer. Every eye in the room was focuses on Mr. Richfield face.

"Keep talking to him Timmy," I whispered, "Your father has been sleeping for a long time, just keep talking to him, I know he can hear you."

Timmy's voice was weak and fading, I knew he was getting very tired.

"Timmy…Timmy"…. A slow shallow whisper filled the room. Mr. Richfield's head slowly turned towards Timmy's voice. His motionless face slowly lit up.

"I knew you could hear me dad," Timmy cried, "Your alright aren't you?" Tears filled my eyes as I listened to Timmy spill his heart out to his father.

"Mary," Janet tapped my shoulder, "I need to speak with you, please go to my office. The ICU nurses will take care of Timmy and his father."

My heart skipped a beat. I lowered my head in shame as the reality of what I had just done began to sink in.

"Where are you going?" Timmy asked as I turned and headed out the door. "When will you be back? Mary, you haven't met my dad yet, wait."

I forced a smile on my tired face and without an explanation I left the room. I knew I had done the right thing bringing Timmy down here but right now I didn't feel very good about it.

My stomach had a million knots in it and my heartfelt like it was in my throat. A feeling of guilt crept all over my face it wouldn't go away.

My heart was pounding so hard I thought it would explode out of my chest as I reached Janet's office. Part of me wanted to turn around and run away another part of me told me to stay and face my boss.

I opened her office door and stepped inside, it was small. Tall gray filing cabinets surrounded its walls and a large wooden desk piled with patient charts filled the center of the room. Two wooden chairs sat in front of the desk. Janet was sitting in one of them. Her eyes were watching me.

CHAPTER 2

"Sit down, Mary," she said, "let's talk." Janet was calm and spoke slowly as she talked to me. Her pumpkin smile had returned to her face. I couldn't help but admire her perfect composure. I, on the other hand was a nervous wreck, I sat down.

"I really like you Mary," she said. I sat up and straightened my back as I listened to her. "You're great with the patients and you have a heart of gold. You were very bold taking Timmy to the ICU unit. I realize you might have saved his father's life, but you broke a lot of rules doing it. I know your intentions were good but somebody could have been hurt."

Janet went on and on about hospital policy and its purpose. I waited for her to say you're fired or please pick up your final paycheck, she didn't.

"Excuse me," I abruptly said, "Am I fired?" I couldn't believe my own ears. I had just interrupted my boss. Part of me didn't care for I was an emotional wreck and I was exhausted.

Janet hesitated a few seconds then said, "No Mary you're not fired. What I want you to do is take some time off I want you to get your life together. You're a very good nurse. Get your priorities straight and when you are ready to work I'll have a job waiting for you."

Janet stood up, walked behind her desk and started reading a patients chart while sitting down.

I stood up and left the room with out saying another word. I felt like a child that had just been reprimanded by the principal, I didn't like the feeling. I think I would have felt better if she would have fired me. I don't know why but everything inside of me just didn't feel right.

I picked up my purse at the nurses station and without saying goodbye to anyone I left the building.

My pager went off as I bent down to unlock my car door. It was my husband's work phone number. Now what? I thought. Should I call John or should I pick up his son Jeremy? I didn't feel like doing either.

I loved my husband dearly but right now my brain was mush. In the short ten months that John and I had been married he had turned my life around.

When we first met I was a frightened battered woman. I was in therapy and I had just left my abusive husband. Both my daughter Katie and I were afraid of everything, even our own shadows.

John turned out to be my knight in shining armor. His bubbly personality along with his loving ways, swept me off my feet. I fell in love with him the minute our eyes met.

Katie liked him too, he constantly joked around with her. He taught and helped both of us remember how to smile.

I took a deep breath and started the engine. Right now, the only thing I knew for sure was that I needed to get out of the hospital's parking lot.

My pager went off again, I didn't look down at it. I turned the car around and headed towards the auto mall where John worked.

My x-husband Larry had never let me drive and although I have been driving the freeways of Los Angeles for close to a year now they still frightened me.

Every time I approached a freeway on ramp my adrenaline surged as I watched my speedometer race from zero to seventy in an instant. A second later five lanes of speeding traffic would come to an abrupt halt.

The death grip I kept on the steering wheel helped calm me as cars whipped left, right and in front of me, this part of my new life I could have lived without.

As I drove, my mind flooded with questions. What do I tell John? Had Jeremy already talked to him? Is John mad at me? Should I tell him what happened at work today?

I pushed the thoughts to the back of my mind as I pulled into the mega car dealership. John's tall well-developed physique and curly brown hair was easy to spot.

He was standing outside directly in front of the huge glass showroom doors. He saw my car and started waving at me.

What a lucky woman I was to have such a wonderful man. His loving gestures and joking ways always brought back my smile.

He met me at the curb as I rolled down the window he said, "Honey where have you been? Are you alright?"

"I'm fine," I replied in an unsettling voice. I held my left hand out the door and squeezed his hand.

"John, do you have a minute? I really need to talk to you."

"Of course, of course dear, I always have time for you." John tightened the grip on my hand, "Your hand is trembling, Mary, are you alright?" John opened my door and helped me out of the car.

"Sweet heart, you're as white as a ghost, what happened?" He pulled me tightly to his chest. "Oh no, don't tell me, I can guess, it was Jeremy right? Has he been yelling at you again?"

I didn't know what to say. Right now hugging John's warm chest was all I wanted to do. I felt so comfortable and safe in his arms.

"I'll tell you what," John said as he stroked my hair, "Lets go across the street and have a cup of coffee. You look like you could use one." "Or," he teased as he raised my chin up to take a closer look at my face, "Do you need a drink?"

"All I need is you right now," I replied as I looked deeply into his blue eyes. I held his hand tightly as he escorted me across the street to a coffee shop.

"Honey," John said, "Lets forget about Jeremy for a while. I have some wonderful news for us."

As John spoke the tension inside of me melted away. Everything that had happened earlier today didn't seem to matter any more.

John brought a smile back to my face. I never believed I could love a man as much as I loved him.

"Can you believe it?" He kept repeating. "Aunt Sara is sending a private plane here just for us. I always knew I liked that old women, can you believe it Mary?"

"Please, please Mary tell me you can get off of work for two weeks. We've never had a honeymoon. This is perfect."

"I've already asked my boss Jake, he said Halloween is a slow time for car sales. So I know I can take off."

John went on and on about his great aunt Sara who was filthy rich or so I had heard. I had never met her or spoken with her. She lived in Colorado we lived in California.

John said she was a party animal until four years ago when her husband died. He had told me lots of stories about her wild extravagant Halloween parties. I hadn't paid much attention to them but they sure sounded exciting.

I sent her an invitation to our wedding, she never responded, I was hoping to meet her there. So like many other new relatives we now shared she just faded into our background.

"Are you sure you want to stay with her?" I questioned as I poured cream into my coffee. "You're the one that told me she was really weird. Can you trust her? Seriously John when was the last time you even talked to her?"

John pulled my hand away from my coffee cup and squeezed it tightly. "Honey," he said, "I promise you, you will love aunt Sara."

"When I was younger my parents and I spent nearly every summer with her. She has this huge castle in Colorado and it's absolutely perfect for a Halloween party."

"I just can't believe she is sending a private plane for us. She used to have parties all the time. I remember one Christmas party lasted for close to an entire week. I received so many toys that my parents had to send them home in boxes because they wouldn't all fit in the car. I'll never forget that year."

John's eyes lit up as he reminisced about his aunt. I listened to him but I wasn't comfortable with the thought of staying with someone I has never met before. It all sounded to good to be true.

"John, I know you're excited about this but you haven't seen or heard from your aunt in how long? What, four our five years, right? And now she's calling you out of the blue and sending an airplane to pick you up. Doesn't that sound a little strange to you?"

"Honey, Stop worrying, Aunt Sara is sweet, old and rich. Just think two wonderful weeks together. Please, Please" he pleated, "Tell me we can go."

John's thick brown curly hair and baby blue eyes were hard to resist. Before I could answer him both of our beepers went off, almost exactly at the same time.

"I've got to go back to work honey." John stood up, then bent over and kissed me. He pulled a five-dollar bill out of his pocket and threw it on the table. "Oh yes Mary," he said as he headed out the door, I forget to tell you, it's a costume party. The theme is jungle. I thought I could go as Tarzan and you could go as Jane. He smiled and started pounding on his chest like he was Tarzan as he turned away from me and hurried out the door.

"Wait! But," My beeper went off again. It was Katie. I looked down at my watch. It was already three thirty. Oh dear I thought I was suppose to pick her up at three.

I grabbed my purse and headed toward the door. My beeper went off again. I looked down at it to see who it was as I headed outside. The message was from Jeremy. My heart sank, I forgot to talk to John about Jeremy.

He was already across the street back in the dealership parking lot. A young couple was following him pointing to cars as they walked.

I was feeling a little bit guilty about not having picked up Jeremy and I knew I was already a half hour late picking up Katie.

Her junior high school was just down the street from Jeremy's high school. Despite how I felt I decided I would pick her up first.

Katie never smiled much and lately she was spending more and more time in her room alone. She was doing well in school so I didn't push her.

My x-husband had constantly badgered her by telling her she was fat and ugly, I figured she needed time to heal.

She was as thin as a rail and her white milky complexion made her look anemic. She hesitated when she spoke and her soft quiet responses sometimes worried me. She never argued or questioned anything.

Jeremy, my new stepson was quite the opposite of my daughter Katie. He was loud, sloppy and testy. He was tall and muscular and he towered over both Katie and I. Lately every other word out of his mouth was filthy or condescending.

He reminded me of my x-husband and I wanted nothing to do with him. When I was around him my blood pressure always jumped and we constantly fought. Whenever foul language began to fly, John usually came to my rescue. He brought out the worst in me.

Jeremy was seventeen and strutting his stuff. Both John and I were holding our breaths and counting the days till he turned eighteen. We both wanted him out of our lives.

Katie was standing close to the pavement as I drove up. "Hi mom" she said as she opened the car door.

"I'm sorry I'm late Honey," I said as I shifted the car into park. "It's okay" Katie said as she sat down in the front seat next to me.

I shifted the car shift back into drive and headed down the street. My heart began pounding faster and louder as I pulled into Jeremy's high school parking lot.

Katie had opened a book and was reading it. She looked up as our car came to a stop. "Where's Jeremy?" She asked as she glanced outside her window.

"You don't want to know," I replied as I put on the emergency brake, I'll be a while. Will you be alright out here?"

"Sure," Katie lowered her head and without another word went back to reading her book.

My hands were sweating, I was really nervous. I took a deep breath and composed myself as I stepped outside the car.

A lot of eyes were drawn to my white nurses uniform as I walked down the dimly lit long gray halls. I took a lot of deep breaths as my heart pounded out of my chest.

I didn't want to be here, none of this felt right. Calm down I kept telling myself, try and relax.

As I opened the principal's heavy wooden door it let out a loud high pitch squeal, it startled me and stopped me in my tracks.

"Hello, you must be Jeremy's mother, come in, come in." The sweet soft voice continued, "I'm Mrs. Motto, I spoke to you earlier today, that old door startles everyone. Please come in, sit down, Jeremy is in the next room."

Mrs. Motto's words were warm and friendly, I hesitated as my eyes scanned the room. She was sitting behind a large metal desk and was smiling. She stood up, pushed her chair away from her desk and continued, "Thank you for coming. Jeremy has had a nice long time to sit and think today. I'm glad you left him here."

"Now, I'll need you to sign this form. Mrs. Motto was calm and seemed quite relaxed as she spoke. Had she forgotten that I had hung up on her earlier today?

"I hope you weren't late for work today dear," she added as she lifted a pen off of her desk and handed it to me.

"Jeremy is a good boy. He's just at that, I know it all stage of his life. Give him time, he's like a diamond in the rough, he just needs a little polishing."

Her words were short and simple they impressed me. Maybe I had been too hard on Jeremy.

"Thank you," I said as I handed her back the signed paper, "Thank you for all of your help."

Mrs. Motto reminded me of my grandma. Her thin white hair was neatly tied up in a bun behind her head. Her dress flowed down below her knees and her thick glasses added character to her chubby face.

"Oh, I know what I forgot to ask you," Mrs. Motto turned back towards me and asked, "Do you or your husband smoke?"

"No," I immediately replied, "Never!"

"That's good," she said as she walked back to her desk. "Honey, he's just experimenting. You caught this early, that's good. Just nip it in the bud, stick with it he's a fine boy."

Her words made me feel a little bit guilty. Had I been too hard on Jeremy? Over the last nine months Jeremy and I had fought like cats and dogs. I couldn't remember a single day where either John or I hadn't had an argument with him.

Maybe we were being too hard on him.

"Oh, I almost forgot to tell you, Jeremy cannot come back to school for two weeks. We don't want him to fall behind in his studies so I'm sending him home with a daily assignment sheet." She handed me a thick manila folder with Jeremy's name neatly typed on the outside.

"If you or your husband can take Jeremy to work with you, it would be good for him and it would keep him out of trouble. Do you have any questions?" she asked as she sat back down behind her desk.

The words two weeks twirled around in my mind. "Did you say two weeks?" I asked as my face lit up.

"Yes, Mrs. Motto replied, "Mr. Terrance does not tolerate smoking in his school. Next time this happens Jeremy will be expelled. Mr. Terrance had a long talk with Jeremy today about this."

I should have looked upset, I couldn't, it was perfect timing, two weeks. Somehow my wacky day just kept getting better.

Mrs. Motto broke her smile and said, "Are you ready for him?"

I took a deep breath, slowly let it out and replied, "Yes." She stood up and opened a door directly behind her desk.

"What the fuck took you so long Mary!" Jeremy yelled as our eyes met.

My smile jumped off of my face as his words echoed through my mind. Every muscle in my body twitched as my adrenaline soared.

Mrs. Motto stepped between us, looked up at Jeremy and said, "Now young man that's no way to talk to your mother, I can call foster care and I will if you don't behave. Now, apologize right now."

Jeremy shifted his eyes from Mrs. Motto's face to mine, I could see fire in them. The room got very quiet. You could feel the tension between us, it was thick enough to cut.

"I mean it young man," Mrs. Motto took a step closer to Jeremy and without blinking an eye said, "Either you apologize right now or you're going back in that room while I make a phone call."

I was in awe of Mrs. Motto's courage, I couldn't help but admire her. Jeremy towered over her yet she remained calm and in his face.

He took a step backwards away from her and then he took a step closer to me.

"Can we go home now Mary?" he asked as he stepped closer to the door.

I wasn't sure what to say. Should I wait for his apology? Or should we just go home.

Mrs. Motto threw me a supportive glance. I decided I wasn't leaving the room without an apology. I plopped down on an old velour couch by the door and I remained silent as I crossed my arms in disgust.

She walked back to her desk, sat down and crossed her arms. Both of our eyes were glued on Jeremy face.

"Alright, alright," he finally said as he nervously tapped his foot, "I'm sorry, now can we go?" He opened the door and without waiting for an answer he walked outside.

Mrs. Motto smiled at me and gave me the thumbs up sign as I followed Jeremy out the door.

"That was real slick Mary," Jeremy said as I caught up to him. "Where's my father?"

I ignored his question and walked right by him. As I walked down the hall I thought about what Mrs. Motto had said. Maybe if I listened to Jeremy instead of yelling at him he would be nicer. Maybe the pain and anger from my x-husband was spilling over on to him.

At this particular moment the only thing I knew for sure was that when I was around him there was a tremendous amount of anger and friction between the two of us.

Katie had moved from the car to a clump of grass close by. Two boys I had never seen before were sitting next to her. I didn't care for the look of either of them. They both had shoulder length hair and were dressed sloppy.

"Let's go honey," I shouted as I rushed out the main door and down the front steps.

I could hear Jeremy grumbling and kicking things as he picked up his pace catching up to me.

Two weeks away from here, in a far away castle with John was sounding better and better. Yes, I made up my mind we were going.

I broke the news to the kids as I drove home.

"I'm not going," "Aunt who?" "No way," Their questions flew.

I listened to them complain but I kept quiet until Jeremy said, "Bullshit, I don't have a rich aunt, this is bullshit."

"Watch your language," I snapped back at him, "No more cussing." I raised the tone in my voice, "Did you hear me young man? I mean it, no more cussing."

"Yes Mary," he quickly and sarcastically replied, "No more cussing, especially from your mouth."

Katie giggled as Jeremy mimicked my voice. Her reaction to his rude behavior surprised me. I didn't scold her because her laughter helped melt away the tension and anger that had built up inside of me.

"You young lady," I said as a smile returned to my face, "you're coming too. You get to stay out of school for two long wonderful weeks, doesn't that sound great?"

Katie looked up at me and for the first time in a long time she smiled, then almost in a disappointing tone said, "I guess so."

Her smile faded faster than it had appeared. I could tell that she wasn't thrilled with the idea. Why not? I didn't get it. If my parents told me I got to stay out of school for two weeks I would have been thrilled, she wasn't happy.

"You're a looser!" Jeremy shouted right next to Katie's ear, "You're a real looser Katie."

"Stop it!" I yelled, "Jeremy I've had enough of you. When we get home go to your room and stay there. I don't want to hear another word from you."

Jeremy kept whispering softly under his breath, "Looser, Katie's a looser," all the way home.

I turned the radio up to drown out his voice.

Katie slammed her book closed, turned toward me and said, "Mom, do I have to go? I'd rather stay here with my friends."

Her question surprised me. She had friends? I had never met or seen any of them and they had never came over to our house, what friends? I thought.

I turned the radio down and said, "Kids listen up, this is an experience of a lifetime. A private plane is being sent all the way from Colorado just for our family. How many people do you know that have ever ridden in a private jet?"

As I spoke I realized I sounded just like John. I was repeating the identical words that he had uses on me to convince me that we had to go on this trip.

The more I talked about the trip the more I couldn't wait to go. John was right, this was going to be fun.

We were leaving Friday morning. That only left one day, tomorrow to plan and pack everything. I turned the radio back up and drifted with the music and all of the exciting thoughts that had flooded my mind.

"I swear, I'm not going," Jeremy mumbled over and over again as he slammed the car door shut. "You can't make me go."

"Keep that mouth of yours shut and go to your room," I reminded him as I opened the front door.

Katie was silent as she walked by me, she starred at the ground as she passed me. She walked directly to her room.

"Wait, Katie," I said, "I need your help. I have a million things to do. I need you to call around and find us costumes."

"Okay, mom," she replied as she went inside her room and closed the door.

"Katie," I said, "Didn't you hear me? I need your help." She didn't answer me.

I walked over and knocked on her door. "Leave me alone mom, go away, I'm tired."

Her voice sounded strange and weak. "Are you all right?" I asked as I knocked again.

"I'm just tired, mom, please go away. I'm going to take a nap right now, okay? Goodnight."

Jeremy poked his head out of his room and repeatedly chanted, "She's a looser. Katie's a looser."

Before I could lash out at him he slammed his door shut and started laughing.

"Honey I'm home," John's warm voice filled the hallway. "Where is everybody?"

It was perfect timing. My blood was boiling and I was about to have a screaming match with Jeremy.

"I'm in the hall," I replied, "and I really, really could use a hug right now."

"Guess what? Dear," John's huge smile and strong bear hug calmed my racing heart. "I sold six cars today. Can you believe it Mary? Six cars."

"Wow, what a great day. How about you and I going out to dinner? Lets celebrate, I'll take you anywhere you want to go."

John stopped talking only for a second as he looked around. "Where are the kids? You didn't throw them out yet, did you Mary?" he teased.

His huge smile and warm loving gestures brought back my smile.

"I thought about throwing Jeremy out," I admitted, "he was caught smoking again in school and has been suspended for two weeks."

"Perfect!" John shouted, "Perfect, Honey I didn't know how to tell you this, but aunt Sara insisted on us bringing the kids."

"I told her how much trouble we were having with Jeremy. She said she could use a teenager around the house. If Jeremy likes it there, she wants to keep him."

"I knew you wouldn't like the idea of taking the kids out of school for two weeks, but now since Jeremy can't go to school anyway, this is perfect."

"Boy this has been a wonderful day. I love you Mary, I promise you we're all going to have a wonderful time."

John's excitement was beginning to rub off on me, I felt better.

"Wait a minute," I said, "I'm confused, "I already told Jeremy and Katie about the trip. I just assumed we were all going together. But we have a problem, John the kids don't want to go. They both hate the idea."

"Why?" John asked, "Katie refused?" John threw me a puzzling glance, "Why?" he asked again.

"Teenagers," I said, "I m convinced that what every you and I like our teenagers have to hate or disagree with."

"What did you say Mary?" A puzzled look froze on John's face as he thought about what I had just said.

"Never mind," I said as I hugged him tighter. "Lets go to the kitchen, I'm starved."

22

It was late afternoon and there was still a lot to be done. Right now I really didn't care how our kids felt about the trip. If aunt Sara was as rich as John said she was I figured she could find a way to entertain them both.

Katie's odd behavior was bothering me. "John, have you noticed anything unusual about Katie?" I asked as I opened the freezer door.

John looked up toward the ceiling as thought looking for an answer. "No, should I have?"

"Mary," He admitted, "You know I'm not real good with girls," He sounded a little guilty as he spoke. "Is she taller? Does she have a new hairstyle?"

Each time John guessed wrong I threw something from the freezer at him. He caught the frozen food, looked at the appetizing pictures, shook his head in disagreement and then playfully tossed them back at me.

"Come on Mary, lets go out, just the two of us. I promise I won't mention Jeremy's name all evening and I'll tell you some more wonderful stories about my aunt Sara."

John got down on his hands and knees and while on all fours he walked over to where I was standing by the freezer. He started rubbing my legs with his back.

"Don't make me beg, woof, woof," he lifted his head up sticking his tongue out far enough to let it droop out of his mouth like a dog panting and said, "Wolf, wolf means please in dog language. "Woof, woof," he repeated as he wagged his rear end as if he were a dog.

"And what did that last wolf, wolf mean?" I asked as I giggled. He lifted his head up and said, "That last wolf, wolf means, please help me up, I'm stuck."

We both giggled as I helped him up off the ground, our lips met and we embraced.

"Boy, don't you guys look cute." Jeremy snidely remarked as he entered the kitchen. "Maybe I should get a leash and tie you both up. Can't you do that stuff in your bedroom?"

"Jeremy," John said without raising his voice, "why do you have to treat Mary and I so badly?" He walked over to the kitchen door and stood only inches away from Jeremy's face. "We're really trying son, we love you and we want you to be part of this family."

John was barely an inch taller than Jeremy. They both had thick curly brown hair and without the peach fuzz on Jeremy's face he looked just like his father.

"I don't smoke, Mary doesn't smoke, what's going on?" John's voice was loud yet calm. He chose his words carefully, "What can we do to help you Jeremy? We want to help."

"I'm hungry, what's for dinner Mary?" Jeremy asked, ignoring everything his father had just said.

"I'm real hungry, how come dinners not ready yet Mary? You always take way to long to make dinner."

"Here eat this," I yelled as I picked up a frozen TV dinner and threw it at him. "Is that fast enough for you Jeremy?"

Jeremy caught it with his right hand while saying, "Temper tempter, Mary has a bad temper."

"Jeremy, you just don't get it, do you?" John's voice deepened as he stepped between Jeremy and I.

"You're out of this house when you're eighteen. That's only eleven months from now. You should be enjoying your new family, not fighting with us. Son, Mary and I love you." Now, go get packed, we're leaving early tomorrow morning."

"Tomorrow!" both Jeremy and I shouted at the same time while a puzzled look filled our face. "What do you mean tomorrow?" I asked, "You said Friday morning. Tomorrow is Thursday."

Jeremy nodded his head agreeing with me as I spoke.

"Oh yes, I forgot," John said as he scratched his head. "The pilot called me a couple of hours ago and said they expect a violent storm here in the Los Angeles area on Friday. He convinced me that we would all be more comfortable if we left early and stayed ahead of the storm.

"What time do we have to leave?" I asked.

"We leave at ten in the morning, I think," John hesitated then added, "No, we leave at eight o clock. That's right, the plane will fly into town tonight ahead of the storm and we need to leave as early as possible."

"Eight in the morning?" I shouted, "Tomorrow? But I don't even have a Halloween costume yet."

There were a million things I had to do before leaving tomorrow. Costumes shouldn't have been on my priority list. For some strange reason they were.

Halloween was my favorite holiday and I wanted to look special.

"I'm still not going," Jeremy said as he rummaged through the refrigerator.

"John," I said as I shook my head, "I can't get us packed by tomorrow morning. Katie's still in school and all of your shirts are at the dry cleaner."

"Who's going to watch the cat and Jeremy's lizard?" I was dizzy with unanswered questions.

CHAPTER 3

"Relax Mary," John handed me the TV dinner to put back in the freezer. "I'll take care of everything. You get the kids and I packed and Jeremy and I will take care of the rest. Okay dear?"

I loved the way John always made everything sound so simple. Why not? I thought, "Okay, I agreed, okay."

"And" John added, "Jeremy and I will start by picking up dinner and costumes tonight. Okay, Honey, or should I call you Jane?" John kissed me on the neck then pounded his chest like he was Tarzan. "You ladies start packing. Jeremy and I should be home within an hour."

"I'm hungry. I'm not going with you and I'm not wearing no stupid Halloween costume," Jeremy complained as John shoveled him out the door.

Tomorrow at eight in the morning my mind kept repeating to me over and over again. I should have been panicking but I wasn't, I was excited.

Questions flooded my mind. Where in Colorado were we going? How cold was it there? What kind of cloths should I pack?

None of the questions mattered right now. I felt safe when I was with John and all I could think about was the two of us spending two wonderful long weeks together.

I turned the stereo on, cranked up the volume and danced around the house as I packed. I felt like a princess that was about to be swept off her feet.

Tomorrow I was being flown to a huge castle far, far away. In my wildest dreams I wouldn't have believed this could have happened to me. I was so very, very lucky to have such a wonderful husband.

Ding-dong, ding-dong, the doorbell rang. At first I confused it with the loud music from our stereo and ignored it. Ding-dong, ding-dong the second time it rang I realized it was the front door, I rushed over to the stereo and turned it down.

"Coming!" I shouted as I hurried to answer it. I hesitated opening the door. It was six pm and dark, I turned on the outside lights.

"Who is it?" I asked as I poked my eye into the peephole. "Who is it?"

"Jeff Morison," a deep voice replied, "Is Mr. Thompson here?"

"Yes," I hastily replied, "I mean, no he is not here."

The man wore a dark blue uniform with a matching hat. Oh my god, I thought Jeremy is in trouble, it's a policeman. What has he done now? My heart skipped a beat. I wanted to walk away from the door and pretend that the doorbell had never rung.

I took a step backwards. The doorbell rang again. "Are you Mrs. Thompson? Mam, are you Mrs. Thompson?"

I didn't know what to do. If I didn't open the door he probably would knock again. If he was the bearer of bad news, I didn't want to hear it.

The doorbell rang again. "Please, Mrs. Thompson it's important that I speak to you and your husband. Please let me in."

Against my better judgment I slowly unlocked and opened the door.

"Good evening, I'm Jeff Morrison your pilot," he said, "Is your husband here?"

"Our what? You mean you're not the police? But I thought."

His tall lean body stood still on our doorstep. His eyes followed me as I gestured with my arms and hands as I tried to figure out what was happening.

"I'm confused," I kept saying. "What are you doing here?"

His thin face remained motionless. "May I come in madam?" he said as he took his hat off.

"Oh," I looked around me and realized I was still standing in the doorway and he was still standing outside.

"Oh" I repeated, "I'm sorry, sure, please" I was tongue-tied. I was still in my nursing uniform and I felt a little bit embarrassed.

"Can I get you something to drink?" I asked as I closed the door behind him.

He turned around facing me and said, "No thank you, are you ready to go?"

"What? Go where?" I asked, "I mean, yes wait a minute, no," I couldn't believe my own words. I must have sounded like an idiot.

"Who's at the door?" Katie appeared at the end of the hallway in sweat pants and a black t-shirt.

"Mom, where is dad? Who is that?" She stepped closer for a better look.

"Honey we're home." The front door opened again. John and Jeremy joined us and immediately circled around Jeff.

"Who are you?" they both asked him at the same time.

"Are you Mr. Thomson?" Jeff stepped forward to shake John's hand. "I'm Jeff Morrison your pilot. Are you ready to leave sir?"

John threw a confusing look towards me. I shrugged my shoulders as I took two packages from Jeremy's hands and headed towards the kitchen, Jeremy followed me.

The smell of Chinese food reminded me how hungry I was. I wanted to dive into it but curiosity about this pilot in our house drew me back out into the living room.

"Don't eat it all," I told Jeremy as I left the kitchen, "I'll be right back."

"When ever you're ready sir, we'll be waiting at gate 65, please hurry." Jeff put his hat back on and walked out the front door.

John was speechless. I don't remember ever seeing him like this. He quietly turned towards me looked into my eyes and said, "The weather has gotten worse. We have to leave tonight."

"When?" I asked. John reached his arm out to hold my hand "As soon we can, Jeff says the sooner the better, are you done packing?"

"Done packing," Jeremy interrupted, "Yeah right, Hello, I just got home. Chinese noodles were dripping out of his mouth as he spoke. "I'm not going anywhere until I finish eating."

"No problem," I calmly replied, "I'll pack for you Jeremy."

"No way!" he yelled, "Don't you go in my room Mary." "Dad" Jeremy yelled, "Tell Mary she can't go into my room." Jeremy slammed the Chinese food container down onto the kitchen counter and made a dash towards his room.

"Where is everybody going?" Katie calmly asked. "I smell Chinese food. What kind of Chinese food did you get mom?"

I glanced towards John to see if he had heard her. He must have, for he was starring at her with a puzzled look on his face.

"I'll get Katie moving," I chuckled, "you work on Jeremy."

John smiled at me and tossed me a kiss as I dashed back into the kitchen to stuff my face.

"Come on Katie," I said, "I'll explain over Chinese food in here."

It was six thirty in the evening. We were twenty minutes away from the airport.

Katie's eyes were squinting, half closed and surrounded in dark circles. She didn't look healthy.

"Eat some dinner," I said, "I'll go pack for you."

"Sure mom, okay," she said as I grabbed a final mouthful of chicken broccoli.

"Wait!" she shouted as I left the kitchen, "Wait mom," she raised her voice. "I'll pack myself. You don't know what cloths I like." Without another word she ran past me and slammed her room door shut.

I turned around without an argument for I was still hungry and the food was still hot. I poked my fork into the other two white containers and washed each bite down with a cold glass of milk.

The food had a calming effect on me, it slowed me down and made me realize how tired I really was.

"I'm ready," John shouted, "Honey, did you save me any dinner?"

"You bet," I shouted from the kitchen, "but you better hurry before Jeremy comes back."

I left the kitchen as John entered it. We threw each other kisses as we passed. "Honey," I said, "Give me ten minutes."

"Katie, were leaving in ten minutes." I said as I knocked on here closed door, "Do you need any help?"

"No," she replied, "Go away mom I'm not going."

"What? What did you say?" I must have heard her wrong.

"You heard me," she repeated, "I'm not going."

Katie's odd behavior was really starting to worry me. She had never acted like this before. A few minutes ago in the kitchen she was talking to me and seemed fine. Now she was upset and refusing to go.

"Katie, are you sick?" I asked, "Let me help you."

"No mom, I already told you. I'm not going I'm staying here with my friends. I'm not leaving school and my friends for two weeks. I'm fourteen I can take care of myself. You guys go, I'll be fine."

Something was wrong, there was no way I was going to leave her here alone.

I looked down at my watch and then pleaded with her. "Please Katie, we can't go unless we all go, that's what aunt Sara said. Please Katie, I promise you, you will have a great time. There are lots of places to get lost in a castle, you will love it."

John walked down the hall and joined me. "Katie we're leaving in five minutes."

His voice had a demanding tone in it. "If you're not dressed I'll carry you on the plane in pajamas, I mean it. You have five minutes to get dressed and packed."

Jeremy peeked out of his room. "Good job dad, keep yelling at her, she's a looser."

John turned towards Jeremy's room, which was across the hall. "I've had enough of your foul language son. I'll have aunt Sara lock you in the dungeon if you don't shut up. Do you understand me?"

"Does she really have a dungeon? Cool! I'll lock myself up. Wow!" Jeremy walked back inside his room and shut the door.

"Five minutes," John shouted, "I mean it, we're all leaving in five minutes."

John and I both paused while giving each other a reassuring glance that we were doing the right thing. Then I headed into our bedroom to double check our suitcases.

John walked around the house closing curtains and locking windows and doors.

I carried my suitcase down the hall. John grabbed it out of my hands. "Don't you carry that Mary, that's a mans job, Jeremy, come out here and help me. Put your mothers luggage in the car."

"Hell no!" Jeremy yelled, "Carry your own damn luggage!"

"What?" John shouted, "How dare you talk like that! I'm sick and tired of your filthy mouth."

John walked up to Jeremy and grabbed his ear. I took two steps backwards. They were both big men. I had never seen John lay a hand on Jeremy before.

"Don't you ever, I mean ever, talk like that again."

Jeremy's ear must have hurt for it was red and he kept slapping his father's hand to let it go.

"You may think you're strong but I will kick your butt if you ever talk like that in this household again. Now, apologize to your mother right now."

"Let go of me!" Jeremy screamed, "It hurts, let go."

"John," I interrupted, "It's okay, he doesn't have to apologize."

"Yes he does," John said, "I'm sick of him treating you like dirt."

"Apologize Jeremy, I mean it right now!" John's arm muscles were flexed and shaking.

Jeremy's entire face was now as red as his ear. Tears were swelling in his eyes.

"Let me go. Damn you, let me go!"

John released his ear. Jeremy shook his head back and forth while taking a step back inside his room.

He sniffled and quietly said, "I'm sorry Mary." Then he grabbed my luggage and almost knocked me down with it as he rushed outside to the car.

I hadn't moved and my heart was pounding like a drum. Katie's room door abruptly opened startling me. I turned to face her. Her eyes were wide open. She turned towards John and starred at him for a few seconds. Then she glanced back at me and without a word she picked up here suitcase, hurried down the hall and slammed the front door behind her.

"Mary, I'm sorry you had to witness that," John said in a calm caring voice. "Sometimes us men can't settle things just by words."

"Are you ready to be swept off your feet my wonderful bride?"

I looked up at John while taking a deep breath. I slowly let it out and said, "I guess so. Are you sure you want to get on an airplane with our two kids?"

John laughed and picked Jeremy's duffle bag up while I grabbed my purse. We walked hand in hand outside to the car.

We should have all been excited, we weren't.

I could feel both Jeremy and Katie staring right through me as I sat down. I turned the radio on and looked over at John for support.

He knew I was upset and uncomfortable. He reached over and kissed me on the cheek and said, "Honey, you won't believe what we're going to be for Halloween. Jeremy and I went to two costumes shops, they were both swamped and the only Tarzan and Jane costumes that they had, were for rent on a daily basis. For two weeks it would have cost us three hundred dollars to rent them. Jeremy had an idea."

"Jeremy you tell Mary what our family is going to be for Halloween." John chuckled under his breath as he said, "Come on Jeremy it was your idea, you tell the girls."

Jeremy hesitated a few seconds then blurted out, "We're all going to be big black hairy gorilla."

"What? What did you say Jeremy?" I turned the radio down and asked him again, "What was that Jeremy? I didn't hear you?

29

In a loud voice Jeremy said, "We're all going to be big black hairy apes."

"Apes?" My high voice shrieked, "What about Tarzan and Jane?" I don't want to be an ugly gorilla's.

Jeremy joined John chuckling quietly as I complained and questioned them.

"I'm sorry honey," John finally said, "That's all they had in the jungle theme that was for sale. Four gorilla suits. We bought four black gorilla suits."

I turned around looking at Katie to see how she felt about being a gorilla her eyes were closed.

"John I don't want to be a gorilla," I complained as I turned back around to the front seat. "I really don't want to be a gorilla."

John and Jeremy couldn't hold back their laughter. The more I complained the louder they laughed.

"Look honey, there's the airport." John changed the subject. "Help me find gate 65, I'm glad this isn't LAX. We could go in circles for hours there."

"Over there, Dad it's over there," Jeremy's deep voice and keen eyes led us to a large red sign that read, Gate 65.

The sign was bright red and centered on a tall chain link fence that had barbed wire across the top.

"Now what?" I asked.

"Never fear, Mr. Horn is hear," John joked as he pushed down on the steering wheel. We all looked out our windows as the horn blared.

A small set of headlights close by the gate flashed on and off.

"What does that mean?" I asked.

"Patience, everybody be patient." John started humming a tune as the bright moving headlights approached us.

Two men in security uniforms got out of a golf cart.

John got out of the car and walked over to them. The three of them talked for a few minutes then all three of them walked back over to our car.

I rolled my window down. One of the men flashed a light on my face as he approached the car.

"Everybody show your ID's," John instructed as he sat back down in the drivers seat.

One guard checked out our ID's as the other one opened the gate.

Jeremy punched Katie hard in the shoulder and chanted, "Wake up looser, wake up looser."

"That's enough," John yelled, interrupting Jeremy's deep voice. "I've had enough, no more of that looser talk, her name is Katie. Be respectful she's your sister."

I expected a fight to break out any second, it didn't.

One of the guards ushered us inside and pointed straight ahead. "Go past that first building. It's the second Cessna on the left. Have a safe trip folks."

John started humming a Christmas song as he slowly drove forward.

"Hello, dad? It's not Christmas its Halloween," Jeremy complained, "Stop singing that stupid song."

Jeremy's voice echoed around the car as he complained, "Can't you drive any faster? I think I can walk faster than this."

John and I kept our eyes on the road as he drove. We both were edgy for it was a cloudy dark night and there were distracting bright lights blinking everywhere.

"Honey, wouldn't it be funny if we got on the wrong plane?" John teased as he reached over and squeezed my hand.

"Better yet," He chuckled, "Lets put the kids on one plane and you and I on another."

"You jerk," Katie screamed as she slapped Jeremy's arm.

"Back off bitch," Jeremy grabbed Katie's arm as she swung at him again.

"Don't you touch her!" I yelled.

"I warned you Jeremy, leave her alone," John added.

The kid's arms flew at each other. Katie pulled her knees to her chest and used her feet to defend herself. Jeremy kept trying to grab her legs as she kicked him.

"Stop it! Stop it!" I yelled, "Both of you stop it."

"She started it." "I did not, he started it." Both of our children were acting like a couple of two year olds.

"Both of you stop fighting right now." I screamed.

"We're here, we're here," John calmly announced as he parked the car. "Don't forget your parachutes."

The kids stopped slapping each other as quickly as they had started. They both looked out their windows.

"It's small," Jeremy complained.

"Mom, I really don't want to go." Katie added.

I opened the car door and stepped outside. Cold water slapped my legs sending chills up my spine. I looked up. Rain splashed and stung my face. My whole body shuttered.

The rain had caught me by surprise, I hesitated a few seconds. This was Los Angeles. We rarely had rain here let alone icy rain like this.

"Get on the plane," John shouted as the cold hard water pounded me. "Mary," he repeated, "Get on the plane."

I reached into the car grabbing my purse then hurried toward the plane. The ground was slippery. My shoes slipped and slid as I dug in for better traction.

"Come on kids," I turned briefly to see if they were behind me. Jeremy was but I couldn't see Katie.

"Where's Katie?" I asked as I climbed the narrow steep metal stairs.

"I don't know, hurry up Mary," Jeremy complained, "I'm cold, get in there."

I felt like kicking Jeremy back down the stairs but I didn't. I threw him a dirty look and as soon as he was inside the plane I got back in the doorway and looked outside for Katie.

I could see John and another person running back and forth from our car to the plane. It was getting darker by the minute. I could barely make out our car anymore.

"Hello, Mrs. Thompson," A familiar deep voice said, "welcome aboard the luck lady."

I turned towards the voice, it was Mr. Morrison the pilot. For some reason he looked taller inside the plane.

"We'll be taking off in about twenty minutes. I'm glad you folks got here early. This storm is growing faster than I had originally thought, the sooner we leave the better."

I felt a knot growing in my stomach. I didn't like what I had just heard. My mind flooded with concerns and questions, I put them on hold for right now more importantly I needed to find out where Katie was.

I turned back around and looked outside, "John," I shouted as I stuck my head out the door, "Where's Katie?"

John was sharing an umbrella with another man. I don't think he heard me. The rain was deafening.

I'd never heard rain this loud before. It landed on the plane and slapped the metal so hard that it made everything around me creak and groan. The sounds frightened me. I felt like I was inside a large crushable tin can. The knot in my stomach tightened.

I looked back outside into the darkness. A light went on in our car. The shadow of a tall man appeared next to the car door.

"Mary," John shouted, "What is Katie still doing in the car?" His voice faded in the pelting rain.

"John," I yelled, "Is that Katie?"

The light went out as the car door closed. I could hear feet splashing in the water as they approached the plane.

"What was Katie still doing in the car?" John asked as he helped her up the slippery steps.

"I don't know," I replied, "Are we really going to fly in this tin can?"

"What?" John wiped the water off of his face. "Tin can, did you call this aerodynamicly perfect machine a tin can?"

"Mary, you should be ashamed of yourself. Don't let our pilot Jeff hear you say that about this plane. He will throw you out of here without a parachute."

I could tell by the tone in John's voice that he wasn't kidding.

I wasn't sure what to say, so I walked over to Katie and handed her a dry towel.

"What's going on?" I asked as I patted the towel on her wet face and hair." Why didn't you get on the plane?"

Katie was shivering and had curled up into a fetus position on the couch. She didn't answer me.

I gently lifted her chin up so I could see her face. "You've been acting awfully strange Katie, what's going on?"

She reluctantly opened her eyes and looked up at me. "I've already told you mom, I don't want to be here." She lowered her head back down to the couch and pulled her knees tightly to her chest.

Dad, this is really cool," Jeremy said as he swung back and forth in an overstuffed swivel chair.

"Do they have a refrigerator or any food in here I'm hungry. Where's the waitress?"

John grabbed my hand and pulled it to his lips for a kiss. He disguised his voice trying to sound like a girl.

"Lady's and gentlemen welcome to Halloween flight 101. Please fasten your parachutes and seat belts. For your viewing pleasure tonight we will be watching the movie Airplane."

"That's stupid dad," Jeremy twirled around and around in his chair, "Where's the waitress? Can I have a beer?"

"Is everyone aboard? Are you folks ready to leave?" Jeff popped his head from the front of the plane and looked around the room.

"I am," Jeremy said, "but miss looser over there doesn't want to go."

"Screw you!" Katie yelled without even raising her head.

"We're one happy family" John's deep voice echoed around the plane as he walked over and shook Jeff's hand. "Yes sir we're all aboard."

"Does this plane have the new GPS guidance system?" John asked.

"Why yes it does. Do you fly Mr. Thompson?"

Jeff hesitated a few seconds waiting for a response then turned and walked back to the front of the plane.

John followed him. "I use to," John let out a long deep sigh, "A long time ago, before I got married and had kids."

I heard both men chuckle as they disappeared into the cockpit.

Jeremy was right about one thing. This plane was small. I'd never been on a private plane before and I hadn't flown much either.

The engines started, sending a loud roar of rattling noises to every inch of the metal that surrounded us. The noise was deafening. It made me feel very uncomfortable. The knot in my stomach tightened.

I sat down and took a deep breath as I looked around the cabin. My heart was racing. My hands were sweating as I tightened my grip on the couch.

"Look who's scared, look who's scared," Jeremy pointed at me while tapping his feet to music.

"Dad," he yelled, "Mary's a looser just like her daughter Katie."

I was sitting on a brown leather couch. Katie was lying next to me. Jeremy was sitting across the room in an overstuffed swivel chair.

I sprang off of the couch and slapped his face. It caught him by surprise.

"Don't you ever call me or Katie a looser again!" I screamed as I swung my arm forward to hit him again.

"Fuck you!" Jeremy yelled as he ducked his head and whipped his chair in a circle away from me.

"Get him mom," Katie yelled as she poked her head up, "get him."

"Dad," Jeremy yelled, "Get this bitch off of me, help."

"Get out of this plane!" I screamed, "Get off of this plane". I pointed to the door and screamed again, "get off of this plane, NOW!"

CHAPTER 4

My blood was boiling and my entire body was shaking. This was my honeymoon and I wasn't going to stay on the same plane with this seventeen-year-old jerk.

Katie dashed by me and ran to the front of the plane. "John," she shouted, "help, mom's in trouble."

John darted past her and stopped between Jeremy and I.

"Ok you two," He looked both of us in the eyes and with a very stern look on his face said, "Back to your corners, both of you."

"No" I said, "I'm sorry John I can't do that. I can't stay on this small airplane with your son for four hours. He just called me a looser and a bitch."

Tears swelled in my eyes as I continued, "It's not you John, I love you very much. It's Jeremy, I just can't live with him any longer." I spilled my heart out as tears ran down my cheeks. John cradled me and stroked my hair. "Everything is going to be all right Mary," He kept repeating, "I promise you, everything is going to be all right."

Jeff was standing in the doorway of the cockpit watching us all.

I was embarrassed, I felt like I had let John down. I was supposed to be helping him with Jeremy, not screaming and hitting him.

My nerves were shattered, I slowly sat back down on the couch.

"Ten minutes till take off." Jeff walked by John and I looking for a reaction as he pulled the stairs up and locked the main door.

Jeremy had put his headset back on and was calmly tapping his feet to music back in the overstuffed chair.

Katie had sprawled back out on the couch with a blanket and her eyes were once again closed.

"What would you do without me?" John wiped the tears from my eyes and kissed my nose.

"Honey, how about a cold beer? Better yet I will make you a James Bond martini."

Before I could refuse John started humming and danced his way to the front of the plane.

On the left side a large mirror curled up the side of the plane. A set of long rectangular dark wooden cabinets stretched out neatly below the huge mirror. At first glance they didn't look like they were designed to open.

John twirled in a circle in front of them. "Ta, da," he said as he touched the end cabinet. Like magic it opened, swung out and lit up, glass inside glittered like ice.

John pulled out two martini glasses and set them on the counter as he twirled around again while opening the next cabinet.

"Shaken not stirred, right?" He hummed and twirled around and around while blowing kisses at me.

"Where did you learn to do that?" I had calmed down enough where I could talk and my body had stopped trembling. "How did you know what was in those cabinets?"

John held his hand out. "Can I have this dance my love?" He wiggled his hips and twirled back over to the couch caring two half filled glasses.

"To us," he said as he handed me a martini glass, "I love you Mary." He kissed me lightly on the lips then tapped his glass against mine. "I'm yours forever dear." He took a sip from his glass I followed his lead.

Somehow once again he had made everything perfect. "Don't you ever leave me," I said as I kissed him long and hard, "I love you dear."

"We've got clearance," Jeff's loud voice pulled my eyes away from John's face. Please fasten your seatbelts" He continued, "and turn off all electronic devices."

John grabbed my empty glass then he darted to the front of the plane.

"I'll be back in a minute honey. You relax with Katie. Jeff told me I could help him with the take-off as long as I don't touch anything. I love you honey, I'll be right back."

He blew me a kiss then disappeared into the cockpit. The couch was soft and very comfortable. I pulled a blanket from behind it and curled up on the other side of Katie.

"Wake up honey," I heard Johns loving warm voice say, "Mary, wake up." I felt his strong hands stroking up and down my arms then he stroked my hair.

My eyes were heavy I was dizzy. "Wow, what did you put in that drink?" I asked as I slowly sat up.

"Honey look, we're approaching Las Vegas. Come over here Mary look out this window. Jeff is going to fly us over the Las Vegas strip. I want you to see how pretty it looks at night from the air."

"How long have I been asleep?" I tried to blink the dizziness away.

"Look," John touched his finger on the window, "Down there Mary, isn't that the chapel we got married in?" His voice was filled with excitement.

"What? Really?" I pushed my nose tightly against the cold glass and looked out.

John and I had gotten married in Las Vegas. The memories came flooding back. My breath quickly fogged up the window, I couldn't see a thing.

"Are you sure?" I turned my head around to look back at John.

"Honest," he said, "It's right down there on the left."

He sounded serious as he spoke but as I turned around a second time to look at him he covered his mouth up with his hand as he tried to hide his laughter.

"You're teasing me, aren't you?" I said as I grabbed his hand pulling it away from his mouth.

"Shame on you sweetheart, I was fast asleep, go away, let me go back to sleep."

John was grinning and held back his laughter as he laid the thin white blanket back on top of me.

"Mary I've got an idea," he said, "How about you and I parachute down to Las Vegas right now and get remarried on the Las Vegas strip. I know the kids wouldn't miss us. We can spend the next two weeks all by ourselves having fun in Las Vegas while the kids try to find us. What do you say?"

John was so serous that I actually thought about it for a few seconds then I busted up laughing.

"Honey," John asked while rubbing my shoulders, "Would you like another martini?" "Come on Mary don't go back to sleep. Please don't leave me awake with Jeremy." He joked.

"Stop it John," I complained, "go talk to Jeff. Please let me get some sleep I'm really tired." I squirmed back and forth on the couch getting comfortable.

As John walked away our plane shook violently sending both Katie and I tumbling off of the couch onto the ground.

John grabbed for the arm of the couch. He missed and flew backwards past me landing on the thick red carpet in the back of the plane.

Jeremy's chair twisted around to the left throwing him forward to the ground, his headset flew off.

I looked up towards the window, a bright light flashed, shocking my eyes with light.

"What the hell's happening?" Jeremy shouted as he pulled himself up off the floor.

"Who pushed me out of my chair?"

"John, are you alright?" I asked as I twisted my neck around to look at him.

"Mom, what is going on?" Katie said as she sat up and grabbed onto the couch to keep from falling again.

"John, what is it, what's wrong?" I grabbed onto the couch and held on.

The plane shifted again. This time straight down. My stomach touched my toes then it jumped up, sending my heart into my throat.

John had crawled over to a straight-backed chair about eight feet behind me. He managed to sit down and fastened his seat belt.

"Dad," Jeremy yelled, "What the hell is going on?"

"Mom?" Katie cried, "What's happening?"

Their questions bounced around the room along with all of our arms and legs.

All of our eyes were watching John's face, waiting for an answer. He remained quiet and was studying the ceiling.

"What is it John?" My heart was pounding out of my chest. My stomach was twisting and turning, I felt queasy. My fingernails had dug into the couch like cat claws clinging on for life.

Jeff's deep voice filled the cabin. "Hang on folks we hit some turbulence. Please fasten your seat belts were going to climb above this storm."

Using a seatbelt as a rope I pulled myself up back onto the couch and quickly fastened myself in. Katie watched me and followed right behind me.

Jeremy didn't. "This is so cool!" he kept shouting as the plane rattled and jumped around in the sky. His body was like a floppy doll being thrown up and down all over the plane.

I should have yelled at him, for not getting his seatbelt on but I didn't. I could tell by the expressions on his face that he really was enjoying himself.

Katie and I on the other hand were white as ghost and holding on for dear life.

John's eyes kept circling the walls and ceiling of the plane in between glancing at Jeremy as he bounced around like a ball.

As quickly as the plane had started shaking it stopped.

"Sorry about that folks," Jeff's voice once again filled the room. "There's a large storm moving in and we'll try to stay above it. We're changing course and if the weather holds up we should arrive in Grand Junction Colorado on time."

His words didn't sooth or calm me. My body felt like it still was on an out of control roller coaster.

My heart was still pounding as if it was waiting for another loop or drop. Every little movement or noise sent my hands grabbing for a tighter grip on the couch.

"Dad, that was major cool." Jeremy was grinning from ear to ear. "That was better then Magic Mountain, when can I learn to fly?"

As Jeremy spoke the tone in his voice changed, the bitterness and anger were gone. He was speaking in full sentences and actually communicating with John.

I remembered what Mrs. Motto had told me, maybe I had been too hard on him.

I pretended I didn't hear him as I turned to talk to Katie. Her face was pale. She was white as a ghost and she was staring at the ground. Are you all right?" I asked as I loosened my seatbelt.

"Mom, I think I'm going to throw up where's the bathroom?"

"John, where's the bathroom?" I asked as I hastily unfastened her seat belt, "Katie's sick."

John pointed over his head, "Back there honey to the left."

"Jeremy, what do you mean you don't remember me flying?" John teased, "Don't you teenagers remember anything?"

"Mary," John shouted over Jeremy's voice, "I want to be a teenager again so I don't have to remember anything. What do you think? Do you want to join me?"

I held Katie's shoulder length brown hair back behind her head as I quickly escorted her to the bathroom.

As we whizzed past Jeremy he pointed at us and whispered something to John.

I didn't hear what he said but his hand gestures were enough to start my blood boiling. Calm down, ignore him a little voice in side of me said. Remember what Mrs. Motto said just ignore him.

"I can't hold it," Katie cried as she coughed and gasped for air. I grabbed for the bathroom door. The opening was too small for both of us to fit through. I pushed her inside while still holding onto her hair. She fell to her knees and grabbed both sides of the toilet with her hands. She heaved and coughed. The smell turned my stomach, I tried to hold my breath.

John's face appeared in the bathroom doorway. "Are you girls all right?" he asked as his smile faded and his face puckered like he had just bit into a lemon. He took a step backwards.

Jeremy popped his head around John's. "What the hell is the terrible smell? Damn that's bad."

I looked up and hissed at Jeremy, I wanted to scream at him but I didn't. I turned away from him and slammed the door in his face.

"Can we go home now?" Katie cried in between taking breaths, "Please mom."

"You'll be just fine honey," I said as I handed her toilet paper to wipe her mouth "Do you feel any better?"

"No," she whimpered, "please mom let me go home I'm really sick." I felt her forehead. It was clammy but not hot.

"How about a cold soda?" I changed the subject as I wet a cotton towel for her. "Lets get you out of here."

Before she could complain again I opened the door and carefully helped her outside. I applied a wet towel to her forehead and held it for her. Her body was limp and she dragged her feet as she walked back to the couch.

Her face was puffy and red and her eyes were hollow and dark. Her strange behavior was really worrying me. I felt sorry for her and I kind of wished I could have sent her home.

"Where's Jeremy?" I asked as I walked Katie back to the couch.

John opened his eyes real wide, grinned at me and said, "He's flying the plane. Any last request?"

Katie looked up circling her eyes around the room, "That was a joke, right John?" she asked as she laid back down, "You wouldn't really let him fly this plane right?"

"Don't look at me," John said almost defensively, "I wouldn't let him drive my car let alone this plane. But I'm not flying this plane Jeff is and as odd as it may sound Jeremy is getting along beautifully with him."

"He's a different person in the cockpit and Jeff's impressed about his knowledge of airplanes. Maybe this is what his destiny is to be?"

"And that is?" I stared at John waiting for an answer.

"Why a pilot, of course. Jeremy would make a wonderful pilot." John nodded his head agreeing with himself, "Yes, he would make a wonderful pilot."

Katie and I traded a puzzled look then almost at the same time we laughed and said, "right."

I disguised my voice and said, "Hi I'm Jeremy your captain, all passengers hurry up because I'm late, get on my god damn plane now."

"Yeah," Katie added, "I would love to have Jeremy as my pilot. We could name his plane the California looser."

"Oh come on girls, give him a chance," John pleaded, "He's just going through a phase right now."

"He's a jerk and an idiot," Katie complained as she pulled her legs tightly to her chest and buried her head under a blanket.

"Keep an eye on him John," I said as he walked toward the front of the plane.

I curled up on the other side of the couch and closed my eyes. I thought of my friend Rhonda and sweet little Timmy from the hospital as I fell asleep. It was hard for me to believe that only this morning I was with them.

This morning seemed like such a long time ago. Questions concerning my job and about Rhonda getting fired whirled around in my mind as I fell into a deep, deep sleep.

"Get up! Mary get up," a familiar voice said. John must be teasing me I thought. I pulled my blanket further over my head and went back to sleep.

Pain shot through my arm, it felt real, I opened my eyes.

Dark red carpet surrounded me. Where was I? This couldn't be a dream. My left hand was throbbing. I realized I was lying on top of it and that I was on the ground. I tried to sit up to see what was happening but as I pulled my back upwards, Katie tumbled off the couch and landed directly on top of me sending me slamming back down to the ground.

My head hit the ground first, I couldn't breath, Katie had flattened me. Everything around me seemed to be moving in slow motion. I couldn't collect my thoughts. My heart was racing and adrenaline was flowing to every inch of my body, I was dizzy.

"Get off of her, you idiot," My eyes followed Jeremy's voice as he grabbed Katie's thin arm and yanked at it hard.

"Ouch," she screamed, "that hurts, leave me alone."

Her bony knees fell back onto my chest as Jeremy let go of her.

A sharp pain shot through my hips then my legs. It raced around my entire body waking up nerves, shocking them. I felt like someone had just cut me in half.

"You idiot Katie," Jeremy yelled, "get off of your mom."

I wanted to scream but I couldn't. I tried to yell to defend Katie but no words came out. I was afraid to move. Every inch of my body was screaming in pain.

I could tell by the puzzled expression on Katie's face that she too was disoriented and confused.

Jeremy wasn't helping. He lashed out and yelled at her as he kept grabbing her arm. She kept fighting him off as she tried to stand up.

I was lying beneath them both, terrified that one or both of them would fall back down on top of me as they struggled and argued with each other.

The plane spiraled downwards sending both Jeremy and Katie flying forward.

My heart jumped into my throat pushing oxygen into my lungs. I gasped and coughed at the same time. Tears filled my eyes. I rolled onto my side and again gasped for air, it hurt to breath, I took short shallow breaths.

"You looser," Jeremy shouted, "you just hurt your own mother."

"Shut up you idiot," Katie kept yelling back, "shut up."

I could hear their voices but I couldn't see either of them. I was lying on my side on the ground facing the couch. My left hand was throbbing. I tucked it in close to my chest and kept it there. My right hand had latched onto the armrest of the couch.

Our plane was in a steep dive we were falling.

I dug my fingernails deep into the slippery leather of the couch hoping it would hold me and keep me from flying forward as the plane dived.

Jeremy and Katie were screaming and crying. I shouted out to them and then I started praying.

"Dad," Jeremy kept screaming, "What the hell is going on? Where are you?"

John didn't answer him.

Please I prayed, Jeff please, announce that this is just a little bit of turbulence.

The plane's metal was moaning and groaning. It sounded like a tin can slowly being crushed.

Please God I prayed don't let us die.

My grip was slipping, I couldn't hold on, my body tumbled forward. I was helpless and my chest felt like it was going to explode as I rolled faster and faster downhill.

"Mom," I heard Katie yell as I rolled past her, "somebody help my mom."

Everything was moving too fast. I tried to grab onto the furniture as I rolled past it but I couldn't.

41

My back made a popping noise as it slammed into a desk close to the front of the plane. My lungs grabbed for oxygen as my neck and arms curled around the desk's legs. I grabbed the desk legs with both of my arms and held on.

"We're going to crash!" Jeremy screamed.

"Mom help me." Katie cried.

"Get into a chair," John's deep voice entered the room, "Get into a chair, tighten your seatbelts and hold on," he yelled. "Mary, where are you? Mary where are you?"

"Over there!" Jeremy shouted, "Dad she's over there."

The plane's engines were deafening. I could barely hear John's voice and I couldn't see him.

"No, no dad," I heard Jeremy yell, "Don't go back up there, stay here, with us."

The next few minutes were a frightening blur everything around me was flying. I could hear Katie screaming, I could hear Jeremy cussing.

I faintly heard John yell, "Hold on tight, we're going down!"'

There was a blinding flash of light followed by total darkness. Then everything got real quiet.

CHAPTER 5

Was I alive? I took a deep breath it hurt. Cold air circled around my neck sending chills up my spine, I had to be alive, I was cold and in pain. But where was I? I couldn't see a thing.

My heart was racing so fast I couldn't catch it. Where was everybody? An awful feeling crept over me. What if everybody else was dead? I pushed the thought out of my mind as I felt the ground around me.

"Hello? John, Katie, Jeremy can you hear me?" I listened long and hard for an answer. I took a deeper breath and tried again, "John, Katie, Jeremy can you hear me?"

The thought of them all being dead kept gnawing away at me. It haunted me as I spoke louder and louder.

My teeth chattered, as the room around me got colder.

Every time I took a deep breath it felt like someone was stabbing me in the rib cage.

I had to close my eyes and lie back down I couldn't stand the pain.

"Help me, help me." I heard a very weak voice cry.

I opened my eyes and looked around.

"Somebody help me." I heard the voice say again.

"Katie, is that you?" I asked as I looked around the room.

I was totally surrounded in a thick cloud of smelly gray smoke. I could clearly see the smoke so I knew it had to be daylight.

The permeating smell of grease and oil turned my stomach.

A million thoughts raced through my mind. Where were we? How badly were we hurt?

Then a terrible thought kept popping up. Was anyone dead? The thought frightened me and it wouldn't go away. My fears spilled over into my heart it raced faster and faster as I took deeper and deeper breaths. Tears filled my eyes as I kept pushing the terrible thoughts away.

"John, Katie, Jeremy please answer me" I cried.

The thick smoke made visibility poor and I could only see about a foot in front of me.

Every inch of me screamed in pain when I moved but I knew I had to do something.

You're a nurse, come on Mary I kept reminding myself. How would you handle this at work? Lets see, of course, immediate first aid. I had to find everyone and see how badly they were hurt.

I pushed myself up into a sitting position. My chest felt like a pile of bricks were on top of it. It hurt to breath but I wasn't coughing blood up so I knew my injured ribs hadn't punctured my lungs.

This was good news. I checked out the rest of my body. Every inch of me was aching but only my left wrist was throbbing.

I moved my fingers on my left hand. They were numb and ice cold but I still could feel and still move them.

I tried to twist my left wrist, I couldn't I knew it was broken. I drew it tightly to my chest and tried to block out the pain.

If my ribs were broken I knew they could puncture my lungs if I moved. Taking shallow breaths eased my pain.

"Can anybody hear me?" I kept asking as I carefully took short shallow breaths to speak. "John, Katie, Jeremy please answer me."

The smoke and the silence were a frightening combination. It made me feel very, very alone. I hated the feeling.

I thought I heard Katie calling out to me earlier, or had I? I wasn't sure but I had to find out.

I braced my front ribs with my left hand as I tucked my knees under my bottom I slowly stood up. I kept my head bent forward because I couldn't see the ceiling and I didn't want to hit it.

The smoke thinned as I stood up, cold air twirled around my face sending chills all the way down to my toes.

I tried to control my quivering as ice cold air covered me. My ribs felt like they were on fire. Each shiver felt like a hundred knives stabbing at me. I couldn't believe that a simple quivering movement could bring on so much pain.

I wanted to lie back down but I didn't. If anybody else was hurt they needed me and right now I really needed them.

The cold air helped my vision. I was sure I was standing in the front of the plane. But everything around me seemed out of place. Wires, jagged metal and broken glass were everywhere.

I chose my steps carefully as I moved around, thank god I had warn my tennis shoes.

My sweat suit felt as thin as paper but I was glad I had it on for it was bulky and comfortable.

A squeaking noise grabbed my attention, it was directly in front of me, I followed it. The medal door to the cockpit was open and moving.

"Hello, Jim, John are you in there?" I listened carefully hoping someone would respond.

The top hinges of the door were missing and the whole door looked like it was going to fall off at any second.

"John, Jeff can you hear me?" I braced my right hand and arm on the cabin wall as I stepped inside. The room was badly caved in. I had to bend my knees and duck down to go any further.

The cockpit was thick in smoke it burned my eyes. A strong smell of burning rubber choked me.

I coughed which sent a slashing pain to my rib cage. I covered my nose and mouth with my right arm and sleeve as I looked around.

Bending in this position caused my ribs to throb even more.

The cabin seemed empty. The visibility was very poor so I felt around the room with my hand.

"Jeff, John are you in here?" I tried to hold what little breath I had so I wouldn't cough.

A putrefied smell of burning flesh choked me causing me to gag and cough even more. My entire body was trembling. I should have left the room but I had to find out who was in here.

Please God I prayed as I slowly and carefully felt around the room, please God let John be alive.

No one was on the right side of the cabin so I turned around and slowly touched everything on the left side.

The odor was much stronger over there. My stomach immediately complained and my right hand momentarily refused to touch anything else.

The smell was all too familiar. I remember it from the hospital. Car accident victims sometimes smelled like this when they had been badly burned.

I transferred out of the emergency room years ago because I couldn't stand its fast pace and stomach turning smells from accident victims. I had hoped I would never have to remember those terrible smells again.

Come on Mary, a little voice inside of me said, you're a nurse you can do this.

My right hand finally touched something soft. It sent my heart racing. I could tell by the way it felt that it was skin. It was soft and gooey.

I moved closer for a better look. My body was trembling and my hands were shaking.

Please God, I prayed don't let this be my husband.

My heart stopped as a head became visible. My legs felt like rubber, I wasn't sure if I could do this.

Come on Mary the little voice inside of me said again, you have to help this person.

I couldn't find an arm to take a pulse. I moved closer to the neck. It was badly burned and disfigured.

I tried to find a pulse, there wasn't any. The only thing I could recognize on the body was the pants they were Jeff's.

His hands and arms were entangled in the windshield. Both of his arms were punched threw the glass and dangling outside.

I felt a little relieved knowing it wasn't John then I became terribly frightened, Jeff was dead.

Where was John? Where were the kids?

I backed out of the cabin not watching or caring where I stepped. I was dizzy with pain and I needed to lie down.

I inched my way towards the couch, it wasn't there, or was it? Maybe I was in the wrong place.

My knees collapsed, the rest of my body followed and fell to the carpet. I was cold, in pain and very frightened.

I closed my eyes trying to forget about what I had just seen.

"Get me out of here. Fuck, where the hell is everyone? Shit, Can't anybody hear me?"

Jeremy's cussing flooded my brain I opened my eyes. He was alive, I was sure of that. I couldn't have mistaken his filthy mouth for any one else.

I was curled in a tight ball lying on my left side. My left hand was safely tucked tightly against my chest.

The blinding smoke that had totally engulfed the plane earlier, was now gone.

I looked around the room. The plane was a twisted mess of metal and wires. My surroundings still reeked of grease and oil it turned my stomach.

The ceiling above me was ripped apart. Numerous jagged holes opened to the sky above and were letting sunlight in.

Broken glass and pieces of furniture were scattered everywhere.

I slowly sat up. The couch I had slept on earlier immediately caught my eye. It was dangling from the ceiling only a few feet in front of me.

Oh my God! I thought if I had been on it when the plane went down I would have been killed.

A terrible thought snuck up and choked me. What if Katie had made it back to the couch? Where was she? I had to find her.

"Is somebody there? Dad is that you?" I followed Jeremy's voice as I looked around the cabin.

I needed to find John and Katie, "Katie, John, where are you?"

"Mary, is that you? Where the hell is everybody? I'm stuck get me out of this fucking hole. Hurry up I'm freezing."

I paid no attention to Jeremy as he spoke. I knew he must have been all right for he was back to his usual vulgar self.

My left wrist was still throbbing but my ribs felt better. Short shallow breaths and non-jerking fluid movements made my pain tolerable.

The sun's rays were a welcome sight even though they didn't seem to add any warmth to the bitter cold that surrounded us.

My fingers were purple and numb and my teeth hadn't stopped chattering since I woke up.

Please God I prayed, let Katie and John be alive.

As Jeremy cussed and complained I inched my way around the plane.

Caved in walls, sharp jagged metal and loosely hanging wires kept me bending and twisting. Every time I needed to bend forward I hesitated because a sharp pain that felt like stabbing knives shot threw my ribcage. It kept reminding me of how badly I was injured.

The thought of John and Katie needing my help kept me moving forward.

Jeremy was very upset. He called out to me over and over again, each time I didn't answer him his voice got louder and sounded more agitated. He knew someone was alive and moving around. He didn't understand why no one was answering him.

Part of me felt guilt for not helping him but I knew I was too weak to help both him and Katie. I chose to help my daughter first.

I tried to yell back at him to let him know I would get him help but my voice was quickly overcome by a violent cough that ricocheted through my ribs like a bullet.

I finally made it to the front of the plane. I walked by the cockpit area, "Katie" I whispered, "Please tell me your alive. Please talk to me."

"Mom! Mom," a faint voice echoed around me. "Help me."

My heart jumped. I closed my eyes and concentrated on her voice. I couldn't tell where it was coming from but I knew it was close.

Glass crunched below my feet as I hastened my pace to find her. It was slippery and I knew if I fell down I might never get back up. The thought didn't slow me down.

Katie was alive somewhere close by. I could see the set of cabinets where John had mixed us a drink. They were pulled away from the wall and their doors were face down on the carpet.

The oversize chair that was to the left of them was wedged underneath the right side partially elevating the cabinets off the ground.

A hand was sticking out from under the raised area of the cabinets. It wasn't moving, I knew it was Katie's.

I bent down and touched her hand it was cold. I took her pulse it was strong. Thank you, I whispered under my breath.

"Katie, can you hear me?" I whispered as I squeezed her hand tightly.

"Yes," she slowly replied, "Mom, please help me."

"Thank god," I cried, "Thank god you're alive. Can you move? Are you hurt?" My adrenaline surged as my nursing skills took over.

My shallow breathing and constant pain kept reminding me that I was hurt.

Katie was awake, conscious and her pulse was strong. That was good. I couldn't see her body or face for she was trapped underneath the heavy cabinets.

"Can you move at all?" I asked as I crawled around the chair.

"Yes, I think so, no I can't. Mom my foots stuck." She sobbed. "Am I going to die?"

Her words caught me by surprise. I hesitated a few seconds before I replied because her words scared me.

"Of course you're not going to die," I finally replied. Then I changed the subject and added, "We're all going to get out of here, I promise?" I squeezed her hand again.

The metal surrounding us was moaning and groaning. I hadn't noticed it until now it worried me.

Where were we? If our plane was to suddenly shift the heavy cabinet that Katie was underneath could crush her. I had to get her out. I needed a plan.

My eyes filled with tears as I squeezed her hand harder. "Hang in there honey, Jeremy is somewhere in the back of the plane, I'll go get him and together we'll get you out."

"I'm so cold," Katie cried, "Don't leave me mom."

I let her hand go and wiped the tears from my eyes. I realized every second now counted. I needed to help Jeremy so he could help me free Katie.

John was on my mind but for now I pushed the thoughts of him away.

Jeremy's voice was in front of me coming from the back of the plane.

Keeping my left wrist tucked tightly into my chest I carefully walked through the maze of glass, broken furniture and metal.

"Is that you, Mary? Please help me, please."

The tone in Jeremy's voice had changed. It sounded warmer more sincere and he had actually used the word please.

I could tell by the way he spoke that he was really frightened. Despite his foul mouth a part of me realized that he was still just a kid, a frightened one at that.

The back of the plane was much darker then in the front. I slowed my pace as I carefully dodged and moved my body around the jagged metal that protruded from every inch of the plane.

My feet abruptly stopped only a few inches away from a large gapping hole in the floor. In the darkness it was almost hidden. I bent down to take a closer look.

A hand popped out from it and almost touched my face. It scared me half to death, I flew backwards and slammed my head into the overhead television.

"Is that you Mary? Can you see my hand? I'm down here. Please help me up."

My head was spinning and I saw stars as my legs collapsed sending my knees crashing to the ground. I held on to my ribcage as they hit the ground.

I closed my eyes and tried to block out the pain as it ricocheted through my body.

"Mary, are you all right?" Jeremy's voice circled through my mind. It helped me remember where I was.

I could feel my body teetering back and forth. I was still on my knees. I wanted to lie down. Stand up Mary a voice inside of me kept repeating, your family needs you get up.

I opened my eyes and looked around. Jeremy's hand was still there flapping back and forth. I looked down toward the ground, held my breath and slowly stood up.

The floor disappeared a few feet in front of me. I cautiously looked over the edge. My eyes followed Jeremy's hand down the opening until it disappeared into the darkness.

"Are you hurt?" I asked as I squeezed his hand.

"No, but its sure dark and cold down here. Can you get me out of here?"

Jeremy's voice was much higher then normal and his hand was trembling. I knew I had to help him.

"Mary," He instructed, "Tell dad I need a knife and a flashlight. My legs are tangled in some kind of wires. I think I can cut myself loose."

Jeremy was quiet for a few seconds. He must have sensed something was wrong.

"Mary, where's my dad? He's ok isn't he?"

My heart sank, I tried to think of something to say but I couldn't. I let go of his hand.

"I'll find you a knife," I finally blurted out, "I'll be right back."

The thought of John being dead crept back in my mind, it sent my heart racing. He's not dead, I kept telling myself as the thought kept haunting me he's not dead.

I needed to find a knife. Where could I find a knife? For some reason I couldn't hold a thought or concentrate on anything. Everything around me was moving. I blinked a few times trying to clear my eyes as I looked around the room.

Of course, I thought, the bar, there's got to be a knife somewhere by the bar. Although it was only about twenty feet from me, it was a long ways away.

I hesitated a few moments as I thought of where else I could find a knife. I took a step forward the ground crunched beneath my shoes. That's it! I thought, glass. Glass is sharp and cuts like a knife.

This simple thought made me feel good, real good and for some odd reason the world lifted off of my shoulders. I knew now that everything was going to be all right. It was a good feeling, a real good feeling.

I bent down to pick up the glass. My ribs quickly reminded me that I was injured.

"Jeremy," I whispered as I leaned over the large crack, "I found some sharp glass. Raise your arm back up and I'll put it in your hand."

"You don't know where my dad is do you Mary?" Jeremy's deep strong voice was momentarily back.

"No, Jeremy I don't," I honestly replied, "But I need your help to find him. Lift your arm up." His arm reappeared out of the darkness. I carefully handed him the sharp glass.

"Mary," Jeremy hesitated a second then asked, "Are we going to die?"

"No," I replied with out hesitation as loud as I could, "I know we aren't going to die." I didn't know why but I was sure that my family was going to live.

"Is the glass working? Is it cutting you free?"

"I think so," Jeremy replied, "but it's slippery and hard to hold on to. I need a larger piece, can you find me one?"

I stood close by the long narrow opening and calmly talked to Jeremy for what seemed like hours.

He yelled and cursed at the glass and wires that had entrapped him. For some strange reason his crude language didn't bother me. Actually right now it was kind of funny listening to him curse and threaten the wires that were holding him captive.

I teased him and then encouraged him especially when he sounded tired and wanted to give up.

"I'm free," he finally shouted, "Mary, I did it, I'm free."

Both of his arms shot up grabbing at the twisted sharp metal opening.

"Wait! I hollered," with barely a whisper, "The opening is real sharp, let me get something to cover the jagged metal."

The opening was only about two feet wide at the largest section. If Jeremy wasn't careful when he squeezed through the small opening, he would be cut to pieces like meat being fed through a grinder.

"I've got to get out of this damn place. It's dark and cold down here. What the hell do you mean wait?"

"Wait," I repeated, "Let me find something to cover the opening with, you'll be cut to pieces if you come up now."

I wasn't sure if Jeremy would listen to me or not.

Stuffing from the inside of chairs was sprawled all around the floor, some of it still had cloth attached to it.

Being careful not to cut myself I gathered an arm full and strategically laid it around the sharp metal covering as much of it as I could.

Jeremy saw my hands and immediately latched onto my arm and started pulling on it.

"Let go!" I screamed, "I'm hurt, stop pulling on my arm, I can't pull you out."

"What?" He yelled, "What the hell do you mean you're hurt?"

I took a step backwards. My ribcage was screaming in pain, I thought I was going to pass out.

"It's okay," I finally replied, "I'm ok. Come on up Jeremy."

His hands reappeared and felt around the opening getting a comfortable grip. His elbows appeared first then his head. His entire body quivered as his arms slowly pulled his long thin body upwards.

I wanted to help him but I couldn't. I stayed a safe distance away and quietly watched him.

His face was covered in grease and his cloths reeked of it. I held my nose and pointed at his gray cloths.

"You smell terrible Jeremy, are you all right?"

He looked around the plane. "God Mary this looks bad. Where is everybody?"

I took a step closer towards him and said, "Be careful Jeremy there's a lot of sharp objects sticking out all around here."

"Oh shit, is that the couch?" Jeremy's mouth dropped wide open as he looked up. "I've got to find my dad."

Jeremy reached out to touch my hand. I took a small step backwards.

"Mary, I saw dad fly by the couch as the floor caved in on me. We've got to find him. He's got to be back there somewhere." Jeremy pointed to the back of the plane that was badly caved in.

I shook my head and said, "No, not now wee need to free Katie first."

"Screw Katie! I'm going to find my dad." He turned away from me and started hollering, "Dad, can you hear me? Where are you?"

"Jeremy," I said as I fought off tears, "I'm your mother and I dearly love your father, he's my whole life. I couldn't live without him and I wouldn't want to. Tears rolled down my cheeks as I spoke. I didn't know what else to say. I was to weak to argue or raise my voice.

"Please help me," I cried, "I can't do this by myself." My legs buckled beneath me, I fell to my knees.

Jeremy grabbed my arm as I collapsed. "Damn Mary you're really hurt aren't you?"

"I don't see any blood, what's wrong? Your insides are broken aren't they?"

I tried to answer him but I no longer could speak. I was dizzy and overwhelmed with pain.

"Come on Mary, I'll help you walk. Show me where Katie is. You're right we'll get her first."

His words were soothing. He put his arm around me and helped me up and without another word we walked towards the front of the plane.

I pointed to Katie's hand as I chocked on my own tears.

"Everything's all right Mary, I'm going to set you down right here." Jeremy turned a chair over that I hadn't even notice before. Then he helped me sit down.

"My tears started my teeth chattering as they kept rolling down my cheeks.

"Hey Katie," Jeremy joked, "Is that you in there looser?" He tapped on her hand as he talked. "What are you doing under that chair? I bet you it's a lot warmer under there then it is out here, right?"

For a minute he sounded just like his father. His voice was warm caring and he was joking about everything.

Katie didn't reply.

Jeremy turned around back towards me and said, "Are you sure she is alive? She isn't hissing at me."

The puzzled look on his face and his joking manner helped dry my tears. I should have been frightened, I wasn't.

Katie's hand started flapping around like a loose fish out of water. Jeremy was facing me and didn't see it.

When he turned back towards her, the sudden movement surprised him. He fell backwards and his head landed only a few inches away from my chair.

It brought a smile back to my face I felt like laughing but I couldn't for my insides hurt too much.

"Well," he said, "at least we know her hand is alive."

I slid off the chair and curled up on a piece of carpet. It was so cold it hurt to even breath. I gathered everything that I could find within my arms reach and laid it on top of me. I was tired and cold. I closed my eyes.

"Holy shit! The fuckers dead."

I felt my shoulder being tapped on as Jeremy's filthy language invaded my mind.

"Mom wake up." Katie cried, "Jeff's dead, you need to help us." Her voice shook with fear as she spoke.

"You're a nurse, get up mom, Jeff needs your help." Katie's knees bumped the back of my ribcage sending pain shooting throughout my body.

I opened my eyes my surroundings were dark, the rays of light were gone.

"Katie, thank god your all right." I propped myself up in a sitting position and held out my good arm for a hug.

"Mom didn't you hear me? Jeff's dead, I think, I mean you need to help him."

I focused my eyes on Katie's face. I couldn't remember when the last time was that I really looked at her I studied her face.

"You know," I said as I slowly touched her hair, "You sure are pretty."

A puzzled look filled her face as she pulled away from me. "Are you all right mom?" "Jeremy says your hurt and I think he might be right."

I was so happy to see her. She was alive and well.

"Can you help Jeff?" she asked again, "Can you tell if he is really dead?" She studied my face looking for an answer.

CHAPTER 6

I lowered my head towards the ground and said, "I'm sorry Katie, and yes Jeff is dead. There is nothing you or I can do for him."

"Cool! I've never seen a dead person before. Is it ok if I touch him?"

I was totally surprised by Katie's response. "What? What did you say?" I expected tears and sadness, instead she was fascinated and curious.

"Damn, this guy really smells." Jeremy's voice once again interrupted my thoughts.

"He's been fucking fried."

I couldn't believe what he had just said. His total disrespect for the dead infuriated me. I didn't have the strength or energy to scream at him. There were too many other things to worry about.

I needed to find my husband, where was John?

It was getting darker and colder by the minute.

"Well, well, look miss sleepyhead's awake." Jeremy stepped out of the cockpit and joined Katie and I.

"Did you find John?" I asked as I pulled my left wrist tightly into my chest.

"Me, hell no! He's your husband," he sarcastically replied, "You find him."

I sat there in shock as I listened to him. This wasn't the same person that had rescued Katie and I a few hours ago, was it?

He stepped closer, "Here, here Mary have a beer." He belched right in my face as he pulled a beer from behind his back.

"You're drunk," I said in disbelief, "you stupid idiot. I don't believe this, you're drunk."

I glanced at Katie. "Don't look at me mom," she said, "I drank the bottled water."

"You liar!" Jeremy yelled.

"Stop it," I cried, "we're family and John needs us. Jeremy, put that beer down, now!"

"No," he hissed, "Who made you the fucking boss anyway?"

My blood boiled as I spoke, I didn't know what to do. I focused my thoughts on John, I had to find him, I knew he needed me.

I shook my head in disgust at Jeremy and quietly said, "Katie I need your help. We need to find John and something to keep us warm. We'll freeze to death tonight if we don't."

Katie's eyes got big and round as she said, "I swear mom I only had one beer. I told Jeremy not to drink, I swear."

"Looser!" Jeremy shouted, "You fucking looser."

"As for you young man," I calmly turned around and plucked the beer can out of Jeremy's hand.

I hesitated, then as quickly as I had taken the beer away from him I handed it back to him.

"Jeremy," I said, "If you want to get drunk instead of helping your father then" I had to take a short shallow breath to continue, "then go ahead. Your old enough to make your own decisions." "And," I added, "suffer the consequences."

I turned and slowly walked toward the back of the plane, Katie followed me.

"Wait!" Jeremy shouted, "I've got to pee, where do I go?"

I turned back around and stared at him for a few seconds.

"What's the problem? Why are you staring at me? I'm not kidding, I really have to go."

Where had John gone wrong with this child? All he was concerned about was himself. Why didn't he realize how much trouble we were in?

I pushed my anger aside and hurried to the back of the plane.

I watched Katie as she walked she was limping quite badly. She wasn't complaining but I could tell that she was in pain, I hadn't noticed it before.

"Katie, why didn't you tell me you were hurt?" I asked as we carefully help each other sit back down not quite making it to the back of the plane.

Standing up and sitting back down almost killed me. I hadn't realized until now that my ribcage moved with almost every motion of my body. The pain was excruciating.

Katie's left ankle was purple and the size of a grapefruit. "Oh my god," I said, "You're ankle looks broken, can you move it?"

Katie looked away from me and was silent.

I bad feeling crept over me something seemed wrong. I knew she was trying to hide something from me.

I stroked her hair, "Hey you, everything will be all right. But I'm confused Katie, your ankle looks bad. I know you're in pain why didn't you tell me about it? Besides being your mother you know I'm a nurse and I can help you."

I tried to make light of the situation. "Does any thing else hurt? Please talk to me honey. I want to help you?"

"Jeremy broke it," She reluctantly whispered. "Jeremy hurt me."

"What? Jeremy did what?" I was more confused now then ever, had I heard her right?

"He hurt my ankle," Katie slowly admitted.

"What?" My voice cracked and leaped up higher.

"See," Katie cried, "That's how Jeremy said you would react, I shouldn't have told you."

I looked up as Jeremy went whizzing by us.

"I've got to pee," he shouted, "don't look."

I turned my head away from him back toward Katie. "What's going on?" I asked, "Will somebody please tell me what's going on?"

Katie glanced back up at me. I must have looked quite confused for she reached her arm out and hugged me.

"He didn't do it on purpose Mom. When he pulled me out from under the couch my ankle was stuck. The only way he could get it loose was to yank it real hard.

It really wasn't his fault, but he thought you would blame it on him."

"Katie" I said, "Don't be silly, as far as I'm concerned Jeremy saved your life. I'm not mad or angry at him I'm proud of him."

"Then why are you yelling at him all the time, Mom?"

After he pulled me out from under the bar we were both real scared. We couldn't wake you up. He found Jeff's body and he didn't know what to do. Beer cans were all over the carpet. We both were really thirsty so we drank them. Please don't be mad at us mom, please."

"You know," Katie admitted, "Jeremy really is a nice guy when he isn't cussing."

"I know," I said as I reached out for another hug, "I know."

"Will you guys hurry up," Jeremy barked, "It's getting dark and we need to find my father."

Katie and I traded grins as we helped each other up and headed toward the back of the plane.

"He has to be in there," Jeremy pointed past the large crack towards the very back of the plane. The large crevice now reeked of urn.

"Did you pee in there?" Katie asked while plastering a grimace look on her face.

"Yes, hell, I didn't know where to go, at least I won't step in it."

Katie and I glanced at each other then we both looked down into the crevice.

"That's gross," she said as she held her nose. We both carefully stepped over the jagged opening and followed Jeremy.

Personally I couldn't have thought of a better place to go to the bathroom but I didn't say a thing.

Only a few feet in front of us the entire body of the plane was caved in. We would have to crawl if we wanted to go any further.

I got on my hands and knees, I couldn't breath, everything around me started spinning.

Jeremy noticed me gasping for air and helped me back up into a sitting position.

I kept nodding my head as though I was all right as I tried to catch my breath. I was getting worse. Even shallow breaths brought on excruciating pain. "Go find John" was the last thing I remember saying.

The cold metal wall that Jeremy had set my back against felt like it was made of nails. I closed my eyes.

"You go first," "No way, it's dark back there, you go first."

The kids constant squabbling kept me awake, they never stopped talking.

Katie kept letting out loud squeals, which time after time opened my eyes. Jeremy's voice would immediately follow with laughter.

Then I heard both of them say at the same time, "Mary, we found dad."

I sat straight up, "Is he all right?" I must have blinked a thousand times waiting for an answer.

"We don't know," Jeremy yelled, "he's not awake."

"Feel his neck for a pulse," I felt blood race through my body as my heart pumped faster.

"How do I do that?" Jeremy said, "I don't know how to do that."

"I think I remember how to do it mom," Katie hollered, "Yes, I'm sure I can take John's pulse."

Every inch of me froze as I listened for the kids' response. Please God I prayed let John be alive.

"He's dead," Jeremy yelled.

My heart sank, my eyes flooded with tears. My hands and arms started trembling.

"No he's not," Katie shouted, "Mom, John is alive."

"You idiot!" she screamed, "You did it wrong Jeremy, his pulse is over here."

A million emotions flooded my mind, I felt happy then sad then I let out a sigh of relief as I started crying.

Had I heard Katie correctly? Wait a minute. What if Jeremy was right? I didn't really know. Was John alive or was he dead?

I had to know, I tried to yell back at them but my voice was barely a whisper. I felt so helpless, all I could do was sit still and hope that Katie was right.

The seconds passed like hours. I kept my eyes glued on the opening that the kids had crawled into. My ears listened and stayed alert waiting for an answer.

What was taking so long? Why was John being so quiet? Question after question flooded my mind sending my heart once again, racing.

Jeremy's face appeared first, he was smiling, I knew John was alive!

"Hurry up Jeremy," Katie complained, "It's creepy back here."

Katie was frowning, the way she looked at me made my heart skip a beat, something was wrong.

"I've got to pee," Jeremy whizzed past me as he unzipped his pants.

His bizarre behavior once again caught me by surprise.

My eyes followed him for a brief moment then I turned around to talk to Katie.

She sat down next to me and said, "John's alive mom, can you hear me?"

Her words took a few minutes to sink in I didn't believe her. I don't know why but things just didn't feel right. I had a real bad feeling in my stomach.

If John was all right then where was he? How come he wasn't talking? Why didn't the kids help him out? My eyes flooded with tears and questions.

"Aah that feels better." Jeremy appeared zipping up his pants. Katie rolled her eyes in disgust as she shook her head.

"Where is John?" I whispered as I tried to speak louder.

"Damn Mary we already told you he's back there." Jeremy pointed towards the small opening that he and Katie had just come from.

I wanted to scream and yell at him but my body wouldn't let me. My eyes were heavy and my thoughts were blurred.

"You're an idiot Jeremy. Why are you always so mean to my mom?" Katie's voice was louder than I had ever heard it.

"Back off you looser!" Jeremy shouted, "She's your mom not mine and you're both losers."

Katie hesitated then said, "No, you're the looser, you're the one flunking school."

"Bull shit," Jeremy hissed, "you're the one on drugs, not me you're the looser. Don't you know your going to jail if you get caught with that shit?"

As the kids screamed and argued my heart raced with their voices. I wanted to stop their bickering but I couldn't. All I could do was listen to them as my thoughts kept drifting further and further away.

Wake up Mary," "Mom can you hear me? We've got to put this on you, Jeremy hold her up," Katie instructed.

"No, you hold her up," Jeremy complained, "She's your mom."

I felt my arms being lifted up on both sided of me. My eyes were still heavy they wouldn't open. A slashing pain tore through my chest. I tried to scream but my mouth wouldn't open.

"Oh my god, Jeremy look," Katie touched my face. "My moms crying, maybe we shouldn't move her."

"We've got to put this gorilla suit on her Katie, if we don't she will freeze to death. Come on Katie help me out."

"I can't lift her." Katie complained, "She's too heavy."

"Okay I'll lift her up while you slide the furry suit on her." Jeremy picked my limp body up like I was a toy puppet.

Slashing pains tore through me as I was twisted and turned around and around.

Neither Katie nor Jeremy was yelling. They were calmly helping each other out.

What ever the kids had wrapped around me was working. My body slowly warmed up. I stopped shivering. My left wrist stopped throbbing and I could actually feel my fingers. Even my feet felt better as though they had been buried deep inside a pile of warm blankets.

My face was covered too. I could feel my warm breath as it wrapped around my numb cheeks and down my neck it felt good.

Strange noises jolted me awake time and time again. I could hear Jeremy and Katie as they quietly talked back and forth to each other. Hearing their calm voices was like a lullaby to my ears. I quickly fell back to sleep.

My eyes opened to total darkness. I could hear birds chirping. It puzzled me then frightened me I couldn't see a thing. I knew my eyes were open for I could feel them blinking, yet everything around me was dark.

I slowly moved every inch of my body, testing it for pain. My left wrist felt better, the throbbing had stopped. I cautiously took short shallow breaths they didn't hurt me, my ribs didn't even notice them. It felt good to breath freely again.

Why was it so dark all around me? Maybe I'm dreaming, I thought. I listened carefully for other clues. The room was quiet. Even the moaning and groaning walls that surrounded us were now silent. The only noise that could be heard was the soft constant chirping from birds, outside.

What was wrong with my eyes? Why couldn't I see anything? My heart pounded quicker as I remembered where I was and what had happened. I didn't want to remember, I felt alone, I needed my husband, where was John?

"John," I called out as I foolishly hastened to my feet. "John, where are you?"

The paid of a thousand knives stabbed my chest pushing the air out of my lungs. My knees collapsed forcing me back to the ground. I braced my arms and hands below me to lessen the blow.

My left wrist made a crunching noise as the weight of my entire body fell on top of it. I took a deep breath to scream but my lungs refused to let any air in. My ribcage felt like it was on fire. My left wrist shook as throbbing pain shot threw it.

I froze my body hoping that by not moving the pain would go away, it didn't. I tried to cry, I couldn't. All I wanted to do was to find John I needed him.

I caught a glimpse of light out of the corner of my left eye. My eyes were drawn to it and followed it.

Oh my god, I thought I'm not blind I have a mask on. Carefully and slowly with my right hand I pulled the heavy awkward mask off.

It was bright out and my eyes hid for a moment as they adjusting to the light. The plane still reeked of oil and the air around me was very, very cold.

I sat up and looked around, I was in the back of the plane by the caved in area. I was covered from head to toe in a thick black hairy suit it startled me. It took me a few moments to realize that the hairy arms and legs moving around were my own. I flapped my arms up and down getting use to the weight that the suit had added.

What a great idea, I thought, the kids found the gorilla Halloween costumes and they realized that they would keep us warm.

As I exhaled the breath from my mouth became noticeably visible, like smoke from a cigarette. I don't know how cold it was but my cheeks were already complaining and my ears were tingling and aching.

I reluctantly put my furry mask back over my head. I was careful to line up the holes in the mask with my eyes. In only a few seconds blood rushed back into my cheeks as my own breath warmed my face and neck. The mask was heavy and awkward but I was a lot warmer with it on.

For a moment I felt good all over. Perhaps the joy of just being warm caused it or maybe because the suit reminded me of the fun I was going to have with it on Halloween, my favorite holiday.

Then a simple thought entered my mind, what if John had bought the Tarzan and Jane costumes? Would I still be alive right now?

Thoughts of John kept haunting me I had to find him. I studied my surroundings again, this time slower and more carefully. I didn't know exactly what I was looking for but I was hoping it was close by.

A dark piece of fur interrupted the bright shag carpeting only a few feet in front of me. My heart jumped as my eyes focused on it.

Was it John? Was he all right? Despite my body telling me not to move I stood up. I tucked my injured wrist under my breast and slowly and carefully walked toward what looked like another gorilla suit.

I felt like a baby standing up and taking its first step. My body swayed back and forth keeping me from falling as I learned to walk with the weight of the suit. My feet were heavy and bulky and I had a hard time lifting them off the ground. I decided the only way I could move with the bulky gorilla feet on was to slowly slide them in front of me a few inches at a time.

A few feet seemed like a mile, a few seconds seemed like a lifetime. Please god I kept thinking please let John be alive.

As I inched forward the black fur took shape. It was another gorilla costume and someone was in it. My eyes flooded with tears as the whole body became visible.

I knelt down next to the body, it wasn't moving. I tried to calm my racing heart as I removed the facemask.

"What the hell, shit, you scared the crap out of me Katie."

I was stunned and I froze as Jeremy grabbed my right arm and squeezed it. "That wasn't funny Katie, I'm going to kick your ass," he yelled.

He raised his voice as he tightened the grip on my arm I was confused. Why did he think I was Katie?

I stared at him hoping he would realize it was me, Mary. He didn't and he immediately yanked hard at my right arm pulling me to my feet. My mask twisted around on my face plunging me back into darkness.

Burning pain raced through my body as everything around me darkened. My thoughts began to blur. I heard Jeremy cussing and yelling at Katie as I felt my body being pushed around like a puppet on a string.

"Stop it! Stop it! Jeremy stop it, I'm over here" I could hear Katie screaming but I couldn't see her.

I tried pulling my mask off so Jeremy could see my face but my left wrist was useless and Jeremy had an iron grip on my right arm.

I tried to speak, no words came out, I was at his mercy. Terrifying memories with my abusive x-husband flooded my mind as pain overwhelmed me I wanted to die. My body went limp and I didn't resist Jeremy as he pushed and shoved me around.

"You ass hole," Katie screamed, "that's my mom, let her go!" Her voice echoed with anger around the plane. "Jeremy," she screamed again, "That's my mom, I'm over here!"

Jeremy released Mary's right arm as quickly as he had latched onto it. Her body fell to the ground like a heavy sack of potatoes.

"What are you doing over there?" Jeremy yelled, "Katie, I thought this was you. Who is this?" He hesitated a few seconds then stomped the ground only a few inches from my head.

"Shit, Oh fuck this is your mom isn't it? Damn it, this is your fault Katie I thought this was you. Well Katie, get over here and help your mom up."

The kids exploded on each other screaming and yelling loud enough to wake up the dead.

Every inch of my body was throbbing I didn't listen to them I didn't care I wanted to die.

"I swear I'll get you for this," Katie screamed as she knelt down next to me and pulled my mask off." Then in a much quieter voice she said, "I'm sorry mom, I'm so sorry."

Jeremy thrust his face only inches away from my face. My body shook at the sight of him and my eyes opened wide. "I didn't mean it Mary, I didn't know it was you. I swear I didn't know it was you."

"Here mom eat this it will help the pain," Katie held a chocolate brownie under my nose then she moved it a few inches away from my eyes for me to see.

"Yum, yum you need to eat this." I opened my mouth she stuffed a large piece of the brownie inside.

At first I couldn't feel my tongue or my taste buds but I knew I wanted more.

"Go get her a beer," Katie yelled at Jeremy, "She needs to wash it down with something."

I opened my mouth over and over again like a helpless baby bird being fed.

Katie and Jeremy took turns pouring beer and stuffing brownies in my mouth.

Maybe it was the brownies maybe it was the beer but all of a sudden I took a deep breath and it didn't hurt.

Katie laid my head in her lap and started talking to me while she stroked my hair. I don't remember her ever talking this much at least not since she was a toddler.

Part of me was listening to her but most of me was drifting in and out of fond memories of her childhood.

Her soft quiet voice brought a smile back to my face, I felt better all over. Jeremy joined the conversation. Occasionally words would heat up between the two of them sometimes into a full-blown argument.

Their quarrelling no longer bothered me it almost sounded friendly. It reminded me of the fights I had with my brother when I was a teenager.

Every time they started raising their voices I would open my mouth and one of them would drop another piece of brownie in it, while the other one would temporarily stop arguing and carefully pour beer down my throat.

As they talked I listened. So many things that they complained about somehow all made since to me now. Although I was silent this was the best conversation I had ever had with both of my teenagers.

How could I have been so blind? How could I have missed all of their problems and worries? I thought I had always been a good parent, right now I wasn't so sure.

Although Jeremy was much older than Katie they talked and argued about everything from their best friends to their deepest secrets.

I had no idea that both of my children were this stressed out. The peer pressure alone from school sounded overwhelming.

They both agreed that the utmost goal in their life at this time was, just trying to fit in. It was such a simple goal and it made mo sense to me.

It was the last thing that they should be worrying about. Their grades, their future, their education, I wanted to talk to them I wanted to explain so many things to them. I needed to let them know how human they really were. I wanted to cry and laugh with them, I wanted to help them.

I realized that my two children were both sensitive human beings and that both of them were great kids and I knew I loved them both with all of my heart.

Somehow along the way I had forgotten that they still were children. They had so many insecurities about life. They needed my love and guidance not my anger and ridicule. I must have been blind. Please God, I prayed as I drifted in and out of their conversation, let me live. Now I can be a better parent, please let me live.

Long thin rays of bright sunshine danced around the plane bouncing and reflecting off of all the exposed and twisted metal. My eyes were attracted to them and followed them as they moved around the room.

The twisted wreck that surrounded me seemed much friendlier now. I was warm and no longer frightened.

What will become of us? I thought, is this our tomb? Maybe I was already dead for I no longer was in pain and I wasn't worried.

A flood of memories danced in front of me as my eyes flirted with the light. I felt John's warm hand as he twirled me around on the dance floor. He was smiling at me and throwing me kisses.

I saw Katie standing proudly in the front row of a college graduation class. She was wearing a white nurses uniform and hat.

I saw Jeremy as an adult. He was wearing a suit and tie and was holding the door open for young eager students as they ran into his classroom. I heard a school bell ring.

I saw Timmy the young patient that I had helped in the hospital. His legs were mended and he was waving at me with one hand and pointing to an airplane that was about to land with his other hand.

I watched school children play and I listened to their laughter as they spun around and around on a merry go round.

The plane Timmy kept pointing at finally landed. A face kept flashing in front of me. I couldn't make it out because it was hidden inside a drifting gray cloud. A breeze came up and slowly blew the cloud away exposing more of the face.

The cloud moved closer and closer to me as the face took shape. The outline of a distinctive hat drew my eyes into it. I knew it was a man's face because of the strong yet strikingly good features that surrounded the thick perfectly cut short black hair. I thought I saw the face smile at me as it played hide and seek inside the clouds.

Something about it was familiar. The cloud shifted and the face changed. The smile faded first. Then its friendly eyes suddenly became hollow and gray while its hair dissolved. Then the entire image faded away like a puff of smoke.

"Oh my god," I yelled, "it's Jeff, he's alive." I took a deep breath as my heart jumped into my throat.

My ribcage immediately rebelled with slashing pain. Was I awake? I was surrounded in darkness. Why was it so dark?

CHAPTER 7

"Katie, Jeremy are you here?" I called out, "Can anyone hear me?"

"What's wrong?" I heard Jeremy's deep voice say as it echoed around our metal tomb, "What's wrong Mary? Were right over here with dad."

"Don't move," Katie added, "We'll be right there."

"Katie," I said as I tried to sit up, "I just saw Jeff our pilot, he's alive we have to help him."

My face was stiff and very cold, as I talked I had a hard time moving my lips, words came out slowly and slurred.

My surroundings were dark, cold and frightening. Noises of the night were once again upon us, everything around me was creaking and moaning.

"Mom, don't get up." Katie's milky white face slowly appeared before me as my eyes adjusted to the darkness. The rest of her from hands to toes was hidden within the darkness of her gorilla suit. She looked like she had been beheaded.

"Oh my god," I screamed, "We're all dead," My adrenaline surged as I frantically tried to stand up.

Jeff's face kept flashing in front of me. It made my skin crawl.

"Calm down mom, don't stand up," Katie dropped to her knees and held out her black furry hand in an attempt to stop me from getting up.

"You don't understand," I said, "Jeff's alive I just spoke to him. I'm a nurse I need to help him."

"Jeremy," Katie yelled, "I think my mom is hallucinating get over here and help me keep her down."

The creaking and moaning that had settled in with the darkness around us was getting louder by the moment. A high-pitched whistling noise kept circling around my ears. It had to be the pilot Jeff calling for my help.

"Katie, I'm your mother let me go, Jeff is calling me he needs me."

Katie turned her head away from me and yelled, "Hurry up Jeremy I can't hold her down."

"Mary, stop it, you're not going anywhere." Jeremy put his hand in front of Katie's and pushed my chest back to the ground. Katie moved closer to my head and with both of her hands she forced my head back down.

"You're all right mom," she quietly whispered, "everything is okay your going to be all right."

I didn't believe her, why was she talking about me being all right? I wasn't worried about me I was getting up to help Jeff. Why didn't she understand this?

My thoughts became blurred as the quick burst of energy I had disappeared. I focused on her voice and closed my eyes.

"God Jeremy, I'm scared," Katie admitted, "What do we do now? I think my mom is in shock."

"Why are you asking me?" Jeremy said, "Your mom's the nurse not me and you're the one that fed her marijuana brownies. I just gave her a drink of beer."

"You don't get it do you," Katie cried, "I mean, I'm really scared what should we do now?"

"How the hell do I know?" Jeremy threw his furry arms up in disgust, "No one in this family has ever asked for my advice on anything and no matter what I do or say I'm always the one that gets blamed for everything, so I don't care what you do. "He stood up, turned away and headed back towards the other side of the plane.

Katie put my mask back over my head then curled up next to me and started crying.

"Is that what girls do when things go wrong?" Jeremy hissed, "You just curl up and die? What a bunch of wimps at least I'm trying to keep us alive."

"Say's who?" Katie raised her voice and said, "All you do is cuss and complain. Now I know why mom and dad scream at you all the time."

"Shut up," Jeremy shouted, "I hear something, listen."

There was a new sound, it was coming from outside we hadn't heard it before. First it sounded like a tree branch creaking with the wind. Then it got louder and closer and sounded like someone was directly outside of the plane scratching the metal.

"What is it?" Katie whispered.

"How the hell do I know?" Jeremy lowered his voice and said, "I'm sorry Katie I'm just really worried about my dad, he still hasn't woken up."

"I've talked to him now for two days and he still can't hear me. I think he's dying."

"Jeremy, I know I'm not a nurse but your dad still has a pulse and we've drizzled water in his mouth all day today. He kept swallowing it so I know he is getting better."

"What I don't understand is why no one has come to rescue us. Jeremy, Do you think everyone thinks were dead? I mean shouldn't someone have found us by now?"

"Katie," Jeremy admitted, "I don't think being dead would be bad at all. You wouldn't have to listen to anybody's crap and I could drink all the beer I wanted."

Katie hesitated a few seconds then said, "Jeremy you definitely need help. I mean you're seventeen, tall, good looking and all you do is feel sorry for yourself. I don't get it, why?"

"What?" Jeremy said, "Did you say that you think I'm good looking?"

"Well, your okay, I mean you're my brother so I really can't tell any of my friends that I think your pretty cool looking. They would all think that I'm weird you know, talking nice about my brother. You know what I mean?"

"I thought you hated me." Jeremy's voice had a humbling tone to it, "I thought you thought that I was some kind of a monster because I yell at your mom all the time. You really think I'm good looking?"

"I think I like you sometimes but sometimes I don't. Especially when you cuss at my mom."

"I was really proud of you during the last football season. I remember the touchdown you made at the homecoming game. All of my friends were envious of me having a famous brother."

"Now me on the other hand, I'm short, ugly and I'm not good at anything, especially sports. I don't have any friends and the few people I hang with tell me that their parents won't let me back in their house. Jeremy your life is a lot better than mine, my life sucks."

"I didn't know you saw me make that touch down at homecoming. I didn't even know that you were at that football game."

"Well," Katie admitted, "Remember I was grounded that night but I snuck out and went to the game anyway. Honestly Jeremy you really should keep playing football you're pretty good."

"Thanks Katie, did you know John in my English class has a crush on you? He thinks you are really hot. I've told him to back off."

"Why?" Katie asked, "Why didn't you tell me?"

"I don't know. I wasn't sure how to tell you. I've never had a sister before and every time I've tried to talk to you, you go to your room and close the door in my face. I figured you just didn't like me."

"No stupid, it's not you, I hide in my room because I can't stand all the yelling. When you and my mom start screaming at each other I can't handle it. I have to get away from you guys."

"Is that the reason you smoke so much marijuana? Katie you're only fourteen and marijuana is some real bad shit. It will get you into big trouble. I know, because I smoked it for a while. I can't believe you brought marijuana brownies."

"Yeah right, like you're an angel or something. I know how much you drink. I've heard stories from Candy and Megan at school."

"Those losers," Jeremy shouted, "don't listen to them. They would say anything for a free joint. I thought you were smarter than that. Don't hang out with them they're whores."

"I know I'm not your real brother but I like talking to you. This is kind of fun. Can we stop arguing with each other and just talk? Why, I don't think you've said ten words to me all of last year. What do you think?"

The room went silent for a few minutes. "It's a deal." Katie finally replied, "I'll try to talk to you if you try not to hurt my mother's feelings so much, okay?"

"Deal," Jeremy said, "hey," he added, "Do you think were going to get in trouble for feeding your mom those marijuana brownies?"

"I don't know," Katie raised her voice and replied, "I know what I can say, I'll tell her that I read about doctors using marijuana on patients that were in a lot of pain, and I know she is in a lot of pain. Do you think the brownies helped her?"

"I guess so," Jeremy replied, "She seems a lot calmer now."

"Listen?" Jeremy softly whispered, "There, there it is again, that noise. It's coming from the front of the plane. Do you hear it Katie?"

"I'm not sure Jeremy. Do you think that mom was right? Do you think that Jeff is alive?"

"Damn, that would be pretty scary if he is. I mean he looked pretty fried to me. This sounds like something from a bad movie. Lets go check it out."

"No way, I'm not going up there." Katie's voice echoed in fear. "If you want to go up there go right ahead. I'm going to stay here close to my mother."

"Chicken," Jeremy teased, "Your afraid aren't you? Come on Katie lets check it out. This could be really awesome. Come on little sister your new tall handsome brother will protect you. Come on Katie lets find out if Jeff really is alive."

"No way," Katie yelled, "He's dead and he stinks and I'm not going back up there ever again."

"My little sister is a wuss, my little sister is a wuss," he chanted, "Come on Katie I'll go ahead of you and protect you. I can't stand to hear that noise all night and if it is Jeff he needs our help."

"You know," Katie replied, "For being a brother you sure are annoying. Now I understand why my mom gets mad at you. All right, all right Jeremy I'll go with you. Not because you want me to, I'll go because if the noise is Jeff you're right he needs our help."

"I'm going to put my mask back on first because the smell is horrible up there."

"Listen?" Jeremy said, "It's getting louder we better go right now."

"Wait a minute" Katie whispered, "Wait, mom's waking up. You go ahead Jeremy. I need to stay with my mom. If you need my help yell."

"Come on Katie. The noise is getting louder and louder. We've got to go help Jeff now. You're mom will be fine, lets go."

"Jeremy's loud voice rippled through my mind waking me up. Once again I was surrounded by darkness. This time I didn't panic. I realized I had a mask covering my face. I remembered the conversation I had had with Jeremy and Katie. I didn't remember seeing John.

"John," I whispered as I slowly and carefully pulled my heavy furry mask off, "where are you?"

My eyes slowly adjusted to my dark surroundings. Cold air immediately slapped my face and choked me as it attacked my lungs sending chills all the way down my spine. My ribs shook in pain as I exhaled, I retreated to short shallow breaths. My eyes blinked repeatedly as I looked around the room for John.

"Hi mom, how are you feeling?" I could here Katie but I couldn't see her. Her voice was calm and it was close by. Hearing another voice in this cold dark room was comforting.

"I'm right here," She continued. I turned my head around following her soft voice.

"Hurry up Katie," Jeremy yelled. As his loud voice blasted around the room my eyes focused on Katie's light milky complexion that shined in the darkness.

"You look better mom," she said, "How are you feeling?"

As she talked to me in the shadows of darkness I think I saw a smile flow on to her face. It made me feel warm all over. I felt closer to her right now than I ever had before, I wanted to hug her and never let her go.

"What the hell is going on back there?" Jeremy's sharp tongue ripped my thoughts wide open.

Katie's smile slipped from her face as she lifted her eyes off of me and looked up towards the front of the plane.

"You stay here mom," She insisted, "I promised Jeremy I would help him with Jeff."

"Jeff? What are you talking about? Katie Jeff is dead."

"Mom, Jeremy thinks Jeff is still alive. If he is we need to help him."

Had Katie just said Jeff or did she say John? My thoughts kept drifting away from me. I must have heard her wrong. She must have said John because we all knew that Jeff was dead, yes she must have meant John.

"Wait Katie," I said as she turned away from me. I pulled my knees closer to my chest. As I stood up I tripped on my own big furry black feet. I forgot how heavy and awkward the gorilla suit was.

My right arm and hand eased my fall as my bottom plopped back down. I braced myself for the shock of pain I felt none all of my thoughts were on John.

"Mary, sit down," Jeremy's voice roared past me. "Katie and I can handle this. You take care of John we'll take care of Jeff."

John, did Jeremy say John or Jeff. "Wait," I shouted with barely a whisper of a voice, "Jeremy did you say John? Where is he?" Tears swelled in my eyes. A flood of emotions unleashed themselves on me as the seconds slowly ticked by. John's alive I kept repeating to myself, keep calm Mary John's alive.

Talking to myself helped drive away the horrible fears that kept haunting me. Closing my eyes for a few seconds then blinking a few times also seemed to help. I couldn't feel tears flow down my cheeks but I knew they were there. Each time my eyes cleared I peered further and deeper into the darkness looking for John. I had to find him.

I inched my way forward carefully and slowly touching everything within my arms reach making sure nothing would cut me.

The closer I moved to the right side of the plane the colder it got. The large metal gash running across the ceiling was letting in an ice-cold breeze that kept twirling around my face.

I looked up while sitting directly under the largest opened gash. The dislodged couch was still suspended from the ceilings twisted wreck. It was swinging back and forth as the wind played with it.

Sitting directly underneath it made me very uncomfortable. It looked like it could fall on me any second.

The open ceiling cracks on this side of the plane shed a lot of light as the moons rays crept in.

Little white flakes kept falling on me. They tickled my nose as more and more of them fell on and all around me. I thought it was raining then I realized it was snowing.

Wonderful childhood memories of snow ball fights and ice skating danced through my head. An instant later the fond memories vanished as a deep dark thought of being buried alive crept all over me.

I brushed the flakes off of my face. My heart sank down deep into my stomach. It was freezing on this side of the plane.

I retreated back to the left side of the plane. As I did a blood-curdling scream startled me stopping me in my tracks.

"What the hell!" Jeremy shouted. "Help!" Katie screamed, "Somebody help Jeff. They're going to eat him."

"Oh shit, this is gross. What do we do?"

"Hit them, stop them," Katie screamed, "They're trying to get in. Mom, dad we need your help."

Katie's voice echoed in fear sending my heart racing. A surge of adrenaline shot through me. I stood up and followed her voice.

"Grab something," She kept shouting, "Hit them, hit them."

I couldn't make out what Katie was saying I just knew that she was in trouble. I slapped my oversized gorilla feet one at a time in front of me and hastened my pace. I could feel and hear glass breaking beneath my feet as I moved.

"Mary, dad help us, I can't stop them" Jeremy cried. The tone in his voice shook in fear as it echoed around the plane.

What was going on? Why was he so frightened? My mind flooded with horrible thoughts as I inched forward bumping into overturned furniture and exposed hanging wires.

I tried to let the kids know that I was almost there but my lungs wouldn't let me take a breath deep enough to use my voice.

The front of the plane still reeked of putrefied flesh and mechanic's grease. It was a horrible smell that turned my stomach. I was forced to hold my breath repeatedly rather than to smell it, I thought I was going to throw up. My eyes even complained as I poked my head into the cockpit, they instantly filled with water as if protecting themselves from the retched smells.

The room was dark, yet I could clearly see both Katie and Jeremy. Katie was standing on the right side of the room a few feet away from me, Jeremy was only a few feet further away on my left side.

He was standing directly over Jeff's body. The stench coming from his corner was so strong I had no doubt in my mind that Jeff was dead.

Katie's arms were waving and pointing at the partially shattered glass window.

"Look mom," She kept shouting, "They're trying to eat Jeff what do we do?"

"Die you suckers," Jeremy's voice ricocheted around the cracked glass as he repeatedly stabbed through an opening in the bottom of the windshield with a long tubular piece of metal.

"What do we do Mary?" he cried, "They're trying to eat Jeff."

Jeff's arms were punched through the glass and dangling outside. An eerie feeling crawled all over me as I looked up and at the windshield. I knew we were being watched. It was a creepy feeling that sent my heart racing.

"Look mom," Katie sobbed as she continued to point to different parts of the cracked windshield, "They're all around us, what are they?"

Wild dogs or wolves kept lunging at Jeff's exposed hands and repeatedly grabbed on to them.

"We've got to help him," Jeremy kept yelling as he repeatedly stabbed at the creatures.

I couldn't tell how badly damaged the windshield was but my gut feelings told me that it wasn't going to hold for much longer.

The wind was rattling and shaking it as the moonlight exposed numerous large visible cracks in it. I could hear movement and shuffling of feet outside and when the wind slowed to a whisper I could hear the snapping of branches from close by.

My instincts told me to run, my heart told me to stay.

CHAPTER 8

"Here they come again," Jeremy's voice broke our silence. "Help me Mary," he screamed, "grab something, don't let them eat Jeff."

My gorilla gloves were too big and bulky to allow me to use my fingers. I didn't want to remove them my hands were protected and warm behind their furry shield.

I could see dark shadows creeping forwards outside the cracked window.

"Hurry up Mary grab something help me, please help me their coming back."

I glanced back toward the cabin looking for anything long and sharp. A second later a crashing noise sent my heart into my throat. I turned back around to see what had happened.

Katie screamed and started crying as four large animals slammed into the windshield and started scratching at it with their claws and teeth.

I lunged forward and wrapped my furry hand around Jeff's gooey smelly arm. I pulled on it with all my might.

"Mary," Jeremy shouted, "Let Jeff's arm go I already tired to pull them back inside the plane, his arms are fried right into the glass. The only way we can keep these animals from eating Jeff's hands is by poking at their faces and mouths when they latch onto his hands. I think I hit the last one in the eye, he really yelped and ran away fast. I need something larger this metal rod isn't long enough and hurry up Mary their coming back."

The pain in my ribs and my left wrist had caught up to me again. I felt like a hole was being punched into my sides. I wanted to help Jeremy but my body wouldn't let me. I needed to do something and I needed to do it quick.

I didn't like the way pain interrupted my thoughts. Every time I focused on how I could help Jeremy slashing pains would overwhelm me and my thoughts became blurred.

"Katie" I softly hollered with the last whisper of breath I could find, "you have to help Jeremy. Find something long and sharp and go help him the wild dogs are coming back.

"I'm scared Mom," Katie cried as she moved around me, "I'm really scared, they're going to eat us, aren't they?"

"No they aren't," I managed to whisper back, "don't worry honey we're all going to be fine. Honey I can barely stand up and my insides are on fire I think I'm going to pass out. Hurry Katie, Jeremy needs your help the dogs are coming back."

Without another word Katie lifted her pale face up looked deeply into my eyes then turned away from me and disappeared into the darkness of the plane.

I turned around and inched closer to Jeremy.

"Thanks for staying with me Mary." Jeremy's deep voice was barely a whisper and it had a warm tone in it as he spoke. His eyes opened wide as he looked deeply into mine. For a second I thought he was John.

"I couldn't say this in front of Katie," he said, "but mom I'm really scared. Do you think we will get out of this alive?"

I could see the fright on Jeremy's face and in his eyes as he spoke. He was honest and very frightened. Tears swelled in my eyes, they were tears of joy, Jeremy had just called me mom. A warm feeling blanketed me I was no longer afraid.

Before he could say another word a dozen beady eyes surrounded the cracked windshield and started scratching it.

"We can't stay, Jeremy we have to leave this room now, the glass won't hold. Run, run, now."

My weak voice was lost in the cracking and crunching noises of the cockpit's windshield as claws and teeth attacked it.

"I won't leave you, Jeff," Jeremy screamed as a loud popping noise caved in the right corner of the glass.

Every inch of me was shaking. I could hear the growling and crunching of glass as the wild dogs teeth were breaking through.

I was helpless, my voice was gone I had no strength. My legs felt like jelly and were barely holding me up.

"Oh my god," Katie screamed, "We're going to be eaten."

Before I could turn around to see her, her arm grabbed my left arm and yanked on it hard. I felt Jeremy push my right side towards Katie as she pulled me out of the cockpit. I managed to lift my right arm up and pointed toward the open cabin door.

"Close that door!" Katie screamed, "Jeremy close it, don't let them back here."

My left hip slammed into the ground just as my shoulder crashed onto the cold metal floor. Pain ricocheted through every inch of my body.

My back was facing Jeremy and Katie. I couldn't see them but I knew what they were doing.

Their voices shook with fear and panic as they desperately tried to seal off the front cockpit door from the rest of the airplane.

The tone in their voices convinced me that they were loosing the battle and that we were going to be killed.

Every inch of my body was shaking anticipating the final attack I was ready to die. Death couldn't be any worse then the pain I was in right now.

Katie was screaming and crying. Jeremy's loud voice was cursing and yelling back at the dogs as they scratched and attacked the cabin door.

All of a sudden everything got real quiet. It was a frightening silence. It was as if we had all made our peace with our maker and we were ready for death.

The only thing I could hear was the whistling of the wind as it blew in through the twisted metal gashes above me. It was a calming low-pitched noise, it sounded like a flute.

I closed my eyes and drifted with the sounds, I was ready.

"Damn, I'm good! Look Katie, hey everybody wake up we're alive."

Jeremy's voice pierced my furry mask and pulled me away from horrible thoughts of being eaten alive.

My legs were tucked close to my chest. My arms and hairy hands were stretched out above me and my head was comfortably lying on my hairy thick gloves.

"Get up mom. Katie get up. Look everybody we're alive. Look, I kept the fucking dogs away all night, we're alive."

Jeremy's enthusiasm pumped blood into my brain. Against my better judgment I sat up. My ribcage immediately rebelled with slashing pain. My left wrist shook in an uncontrollable spasm of pain as I used it to push my body upwards.

I could see daylight from inside my mask it was a welcome sight.

"Mary, Mary where are you?" It was John's voice he was alive. I threw off my hairy gloves and quickly pulled off my heavy furry mask.

The bright light blinded me. I closed my eyes and repeatedly opened them slowly as they adjusted to the brightness around me.

I wasn't sure how long I had been in darkness, right now it didn't matter, John was alive and talking.

My eyes frantically searched around the cabin for him. Why couldn't I see him? My heart was pumping blood so quickly I felt it all the way down in my toes.

"Mary," Jeremy yelled, "you look good I mean, mom you look good." Jeremy hadn't shut his mouth since the minute I opened my eyes. He sounded tired, I paid no attention to him.

Every inch of my body and soul were focused on finding John. The smoke that had blinded us earlier was almost gone. Our surroundings were a lot friendlier looking now.

"Mom, over here dad's right here." Katie's arm drew me to the back of plane past the huge gash in the floor. "Dad's awake, can you walk back here?"

Her voice was music to my ears. Walk? Was she kidding? I was ready to run.

My heart was already flying. I repeatedly tried to pull myself up onto my knees but I couldn't, I couldn't feel my legs. A stabbing pain kept slashing through my lower back and I couldn't stand. I could barely hold myself up in a sitting position.

"Help, Jeremy please help me," I pleaded as I coughed up blood. I felt my body loosing it's balance and as quick as I had sat up I fell back down I couldn't breath, everything around me went dark.

I remembered when John and I first met. His warm smile and bubbly personality immediately attracted me to him.

I bumped into each other while folding cloths in our apartments laundry room one gloomy Saturday afternoon.

He was so charming and handsome I couldn't take my eyes or ears away from him. That gloomy day turned into a candlelight dinner and before I knew it he had swept me off of my feet.

I didn't know that I could ever be this happy. I felt like I had been given a second chance in life I knew we were made for each other. He respected me and encouraged me to become more independent. He made me feel so very special. He was the opposite of my x-husband Larry.

Larry had criticized and belittled me since the day we were married. He never let me out of his sight and when we went out in public he always embarrassed me.

At home I was afraid of him and although he had never hit me, he threatened to many, many a time. I kept to myself and didn't talk to anyone or do much of anything without his permission.

When Katie was born I was hoping it would make him happier. Instead his rage and anger deepened as she grew up. We both were afraid of our own shadows when he was around us.

Leaving him was the hardest and best thing I had ever done. If Larry hadn't made Katie cry so much I probably would have stayed with him.

Going back to work and months of counseling slowly pulled me out of my shattered shell.

I remember how big and frightening the world looked when Katie and I moved out. At first I missed being yelled at and scolded by Larry for everything I did. Then slowly ever so slowly as Katie and I ventured outside of our apartment we realized that there was a big wonderful world out there and that most people in it weren't mean or cruel.

Finding John was a turning point in my life. I felt guilty talking to him so much about my terrible past. He never complained and after dating for a couple of weeks he started spilling out his heart to me telling me lots of horrible stories about his x-wife.

She reminded me a lot of my x-husband. John said she was always cutting him down or cussing at him and his son and she drank like a fish.

I couldn't imagine being so mean to such a loving person. John said the doctors had diagnosed her years ago as a manic depressant. She constantly accused him of what ever her sick mind could dream up during the day while he was away working.

He said he felt obligated to stay with her for they had a son together and until Jeremy turned eighteen he felt he had no other choice.

His life sounded like an emotional roller coaster that was out of control. He finally left her after coming home from work one day and being confronted by a knife and wild accusations of being married to a second person.

The judge awarded custody of Jeremy to his father, John. Like me he was also overwhelmed with his new life. When we met we instantly knew we were made for each other.

Jeremy was polite and quiet when I first met him. A few months after John and I got married he changed. He became bitter and did everything he could to break John and I up he knew how to upset me. His filthy mouth brought out the worst in me.

Katie on the other hand liked John and seemed to adjust to her new life quite easily. She was quiet, sometimes too quiet but when she talked to John she seemed comfortable and happy.

John was my new beginning and I desperately needed him and I truly loved him with all my heart.

"I got you Mary, don't you fucking die on me now. I've been up all night saving you. Wake up."

Light once again overwhelmed my eyes as they slowly opened. Jeremy's curly brown hair and dark green eyes were only a few inches away from my face.

His gorilla mask was off and he was smiling. It looked out of place on his face.

I blinked again and my blurry surroundings came in focus.

"You aren't going to die on me now are you mom?" he said, "I mean that would really suck. It's your turn to keep these wild dogs away I'm really tired, wake up."

I had forgotten how quickly Jeremy could make my blood boil. One moment I felt like slapping him then a second later I wanted to thank him for helping me. I had no energy and my broken body was lifeless all I could was force a smile to my face.

"Katie, mom's awake," Jeremy shouted, "How is my dad doing?"

"I don't know," Katie slowly replied, "He was awake a minute ago but now he won't talk to me and his head is still bleeding. What should we do?"

"How the fuck do I know? I'm tired and hungry and sick of being here."

Jeremy was kneeling next to me as he lashed out at Katie, again I wanted to slap him but my body wouldn't move. How could anyone be this selfish, I thought. Why didn't this kid realize how much we needed him? I needed John, I needed to talk to Katie, I had to do something.

"John please, Katie," My words were barely a whisper and not heard.

I realized I was drifting in and out of consciousness. I knew it was a bad sign but I liked it because it helped the pain go away.

"Oh no you don't, wake up Mary. You're a nurse you have to help my dad, wake up." Jeremy's cold hand slapped my cheek shattering my peace and quiet. "Stay awake Mary, I mean it you need to get up and help my dad."

My eyes opened and were drawn to the ceiling where the large open gash in the twisted metal was.

"You ass," Katie shouted, "don't you ever slap my mom again, get away from her."

I felt like I was being watched. No, I knew I was being watched. An eerie feeling crept all over me and made my skin crawl, my heart started to pound.

I could hear the pitter patter of feet above me. They weren't human and they didn't sound friendly.

Jeremy and Katie were yelling so loudly back and forth at each other that they couldn't hear them.

The wild dogs were back and this time they were above us. The couch that was still dangling from the ceiling and now it looked like a convenient stairway for the dogs to get down to us.

Oh my god, I thought, I can't move or talk. How do I warn the kids?

"You bitch," "You asshole," Both kids were lashing out and screaming at each other as loud as their tired voices would let them.

I could feel my fingers on my right hand. I turned my neck around as far as I could to see them. They were purple, swollen and very stiff but they moved.

There was an empty beer bottle a few inches away from them. I stretched them out and pulled my body as far as it would let me to the right, as I struggled to reach it.

I needed to get Jeremy's and Katie's attention, our lives depended on it. If I could pick this bottle up and throw it, it might break up their fight.

Come on fingers just a little further you can do it, I kept repeating to myself. My fingers were numb I could feel movement in them but I was having a hard time closing them tight enough around the bottle to lift it. I knew my hand was touching it but it was hard knowing how many fingers had latched onto it.

Come on, come on I repeated to myself as my eyes jumped back and forth from the bottle to the ceiling as I struggled for a better grip.

A loud deep growl shot adrenaline threw me and jumpstarted my heart like a flash of lightening.

My right arm shot straight up and flung the bottle over my body I heard it crash.

"What the hell? Where did that come from?"

"Shut up Katie, listen." The room got quiet. The ceiling came alive with scratching and growling noises.

"The dogs are back," Jeremy yelled, "Katie help me get your mom back with my dad. We need to move her away from that couch right now."

I was scared but for some strange reason I felt good inside as Jeremy grabbed my legs and Katie grabbed onto my arms.

Fright was written all over both of their tired faces. I wanted to let them know that everything was going to be all right so I kept a smile plastered on my face.

I closed my eyes and dreamt about dancing with John as I was twisted and pulled around the room like a heavy sack of potatoes.

"Hang in there Mom," Jeremy's voice once again had a warm tone to it, "I won't let them eat you. Come on Katie hurry up."

"Jeremy," Katie asked, "How do we get mom past that big crack in the back of the plane? I can't lift her she's to heavy, the metal will cut her."

"Over there get that couch cushion put it down over the smallest gash. I'll drag her over it, hurry up Katie, hurry." There was alarm and panic in Jeremy's voice as it echoed around the plane.

I kept a smile plastered on my face it was all I had left as encouragement. It took every ounce of energy I had left to keep it in place as they twisted and pulled my broken body.

"Katie, why is your mom smiling? Is she dying? I mean, I know this must be hurting her, do you think she is okay?"

My smile had confused Jeremy and for a split second I felt like laughing.

"I don't think she's dying." Katie replied, "I think she is happy that John is alive. What do we do now?"

Jeremy put his cold hand on my numb red face and stroked my cheeks. "Mom," he said, "I'm sorry, if we live through this I promise I won't cuss at you ever again."

My eyes opened and tears roll down my cheeks as I closely examined his face. Then he softly whispered close to my ear, "Mom, you take care of dad for me and I'll take care of Katie for you, okay?"

I blinked my eyes and held them shut for a few seconds. Jeremy understood me he gestured back by doing the same then he smiled at me. It was the biggest brightest smile I had ever seen.

"What do I do?" Katie repeatedly asked. "Jeremy what am I suppose to do?"

Jeremy stood up, glanced around the room then smiled at Katie. "Little sister" He replied as he yawned, "you have to keep me awake. Yes that's it, you have to keep me from falling asleep, okay?"

"How do I do that? I don't know how to keep you awake. I don't have any coffee or pills so what do I do? How do I keep you awake?"

Jeremy yawned again then replied, "Just keep asking me questions like you are right now. If I don't answer you then kick me or cuss at me. Call me some of the mean names you did earlier they sure pissed me off and woke me up, okay?"

Katie's puzzled expression on her face deepened, "What? What did you say? Cuss at you? Are you crazy?"

Jeremy turned all the way around to look at Katie, "Good job sis keep the questions coming."

He had a plan and he was right about one thing, Katie had been asking him lots of questions. I hadn't heard her speak this much since she was a little girl.

My x-husband Larry had an explosive temper and when he was home Katie would run to her room and hide. She had stopped talking almost all together by her third birthday. Both of us learned to keep quiet and stay out of Larry's way.

Hearing her ask Jeremy the same questions over and over again brought back memories. I liked hearing her voice it reminded me of when she was two years old and every other word out of her mouth was, "why". It helped calm the fear growing inside of me as the scratching and howling outside got louder and more vicious.

"Mary, honey is that you?" I felt a pat on the back of my furry suit it was John. My entire body immediately reacted and somehow I managed to roll over on my side. My nose stopped my face as it touched the carpet, my eyes opened wide and fell upon John's battered face.

His eyes were closed and his face was motionless, I tried to speak to him. I could feel my lips moving but no words came out.

I was afraid if I blinked he would disappear again so I glued my eyes onto his face and forced them to stay open, he opened his eyes.

I had so much to tell him I had missed him so very much.

No, a little voice inside of me said, don't try to talk John will understand you, keep looking at him he will understand you. Blink your eyes at him you must keep him awake.

Thoughts flew in and out of my head as I blinked and watched John. He too remained silent but his eyes stayed open and were only a few inches away from mine. I could feel his warm breath on my face. I wanted to stretch my neck out a few more inches and touched his lips I wanted to kiss him.

His face was terribly swollen and thick dried blood curled around his forehead and ran down past his neck.

I tried not to look at it, it frightened me. It brought back memories of the patients I had treated in the hospital. Every time my eyes glanced at it my thoughts would turn to fear.

I knew that I had to stay awake. I knew I had to help John stay awake.

Sometimes his eyes were wide open other times they were almost closed. Once they looked so hollow I cried, blinking helped to keep me awake.

I had landed on a thick piece of carpet that was soft and comfortable. Neither John nor I had our furry mask on. We were in the back of the plane past the large gash in the floor, I felt safe.

Don't fall asleep, a little voice inside of me kept reminding me keep your eyes open. You have to stay awake.

Jeremy and Katie's voices faded into the background as my eyes joined with John's. We became one, when his eyes moved mine moved, when his eyes blinked mine blinked.

As the sun's rays disappeared our surroundings once more entombed us in an ice-cold darkness.

The scratching and growling from outside hadn't stopped it kept us all on edge. None of the wild dogs had dared to climb down the couch yet but we expected them to try to at any moment.

The ear piercing scratching and gnawing noises got louder and riotous. When the noise was unbearable it would all stop at once as if orchestrated, leaving us listening to our pounding hearts as we strained our ears to hear more. Had they gone? Or were they going to attack us now. The silence was long, cold and frightening.

Jeremy had left his gorilla mask off exposing his curly brown hair to the icy air.

"Jeremy, why haven't you put your mask on? Put it back on, you'll freeze if you don't."

"Shhh Katie listen I think they're leaving. I can't hear with the mask on, be real quiet and listen."

You could have heard a pin drop as the seconds slowly ticked by. Katie followed Jeremy's lead and without a peep she carefully pulled her head mask off and set it down.

If either of them were breathing you wouldn't have noticed. A deep silence blanketed the room as they listened intently. Neither spoke as they scanned the room in different directions listening for sounds.

"We did it, Katie" Jeremy finally whispered, "I think they gave up. We did it."

"Then why are we whispering?" Katie cautiously asked, "Are you sure?"

Jeremy hesitated a few seconds then in a loud masculine voice replied, "Yes little sister I'm sure we're safe, the wild dogs are gone."

His deep voice echoed around the cold metal walls slicing through the silence that had crept in.

"I'm still scared," Katie admitted, "How come no one has rescued us? I mean it Jeremy, I'm really frightened, what do we do now?"

"Thank you," Jeremy replied as he yawned long and hard, "Thank you Katie for keeping me awake. I'm so tired I think I forgot how to sleep. Damn, I've never stayed awake two nights in a row before or has it been three? Lets have a beer to celebrate."

"I'm not thirsty," Katie whimpered, "I'm cold and tired. If you drink beer you will have to go to the bathroom and I'm not going to watch you pee in here again."

"Jeremy, put the beer down." Katie's tiny voice was strained and higher then normal as Jeremy opened the can.

"You know," Jeremy said, "Katie, you and your mom are both alike all you do is bitch. Bitch, bitch, bitch."

"Back off, I'm thirsty and I'm just as tired as you are, so just back off." He raised the beer can up as if he was proposing a toast then turned it upside down and inhaled it.

"Aahh," he sighed as he let out a loud belch, "That's much better. Katie are you sure you don't want one of these, they're really good."

"You know Jeremy, a while ago I thought I liked you. I mean I thought you and I might really end up being good friends. Now I realize how disgusting you really are. All you do is complain and cuss at my mom. I don't want you for a brother I hope I never see you again."

Jeremy picked up another beer, shook it hard then pointed it at Katie and opened it. It shot out a stream of wet foam that flew all over her furry suit.

"You ass hole," She screamed, "You are so immature, no wonder you don't have a girlfriend."

"Looks who's talking," Jeremy said as he drank the rest of the open can, "Miss marijuana brownie dope head."

"I hate you," Katie yelled, "I wish you were dead."

"Screw you," Jeremy screamed back, "I'm the one that saved your ass and now your being a total bitch."

As the screaming match continued neither noticed the noises from outside. The wild dogs had returned and one of them had crouched his body down on the upper part of the hanging couch in an attempt to crawl down it.

As he inched downwards, a gust of wind shot inside the cabin setting the couch into a swinging motion.

The dog stood up as he dug into the couch with his claws. His head slammed into a piece of jagged metal. He let out a loud cry that stopped Katie and Jeremy in their tracks, Katie looked up.

"Oh my god," she cried, "the dogs are back. Oh my god they're almost inside. Do something Jeremy, do something."

Jeremy dropped the can of beer in his hand and slowly looked up. He was standing directly under the couch.

"Do something," Katie screamed again, "Jeremy do something."

Jeremy stood frozen as the four-legged creature crouched back down and exposed his long sharp teeth. He slowly backed off the couch leaving a trail of blood and fur on the twisted metal above.

"Didn't you hear me," Katie screamed.

"Shut up," Jeremy replied, "Just shut up I've got to think a second." Jeremy backed away from the couch and moved closer to Katie.

The sun had set and the sounds of darkness were creeping in.

"Damn, Katie did you see the size of his teeth? They were huge."

"What does that have to do with a plan?" Katie asked, "Are you drunk or something?"

Jeremy mumbled something back at Katie, "What did you say? Oh my god, you are drunk." Katie shook her head in disgust then started crying, "We're going to die I just know it I don't want to be eaten. Please, please, Jeremy help us."

Jeremy turned towards Katie held out his furry arm and said, "They'll have to kill me first Katie, I promise I'll protect you."

Katie's face flooded with tears as she grabbed Jeremy's furry suit for a hug, she held on tight.

"It's okay" Jeremy kept repeating, "We'll be fine I promise you."

Katie's tears turned to sniffles then silence as her pale face laid on Jeremy's hairy chest.

A gust of wind woke up the haunting noises of twisted metal and broken glass.

"It's getting dark in here," Katie said as she wiped her tears away. Shouldn't we put our mask back on?"

She looked up at Jeremy's brown eyes and said, "I'm sorry I didn't mean what I said earlier about you."

Jeremy patted her on the head, smiled and said, "It's okay little sister, I didn't mean to call you a pot head, either."

As the wind whistled through the gashes and twisted metal the noises from above them constantly changed. Sometimes the wild animals howled in tune with each other, occasionally the howling turned to terrifying cries that sounded like the dogs were killing each other. None of the noises were friendly and they repeatedly stopped and without warning, would start again a few minutes later.

In the dead of night the wind died down and everything got real quiet, the silence was frightening. Jeremy and Katie's hearts were racing as they anticipated the worst. Their eyes were focused on the couch gently swinging above them. Katie stepped behind Jeremy, they both knew it was time.

Round beady eyes appeared circling up and down the large gash in the ceiling above them.

The metal that surrounded them came alive. It screamed and sounded like fingernails scratching a chalkboard. It was a horrible sound that ricocheted and echoed off of every exposed inch of metal on the plane.

Jeremy and Katie covered their ears as they watched the eyes above them.

"I can't stand the noise," Katie cried, "Make it go away, Jeremy please make it go away."

"Katie, give me your cigarette lighter." Jeremy reached his left hand back towards Katie without turning around.

"What? What for? Katie questioned as she dug into her pocket.

"Just give it to me," Jeremy yelled, "Now."

The leader of the pack that had attempted to climb down the couch earlier was back, his head and mouth were covered in blood. His fur was dark and matted with gray highlights around his face that reflected in the moonlight.

He looked like any medium sized dog but the fire in his eyes and the blood in his mouth were quite convincing, he wasn't a pet.

Jeremy flicked the lighter on as the dog crouched down and cautiously positioned himself on the end of the couch. He raised his lip and growled exposing razor sharp bloody teeth. Crawling on his stomach he slowly slithered down the couch.

"Kill him," Katie Yelled as she pushed Jeremy forward, "kill him."

A large piece of the sofa stuffing was dangling down from the arm of the sofa. It was within Jeremy's reach. He jumped up and flicked the lighter at it.

"Oh my god," Katie screamed, "What are you doing? We'll all die don't start a fire. Stop it Jeremy, stop it."

CHAPTER 9

It was too late. On his third attempt the puffy white cotton caught fire and like a thirsty dry cloth it quickly sucked up the fire and spread it upwards.

Smoke filled the cabin and the oily burned smell that had engulfed the plane earlier returned.

"Get back," Jeremy screamed, "Katie, get out of here."

"No," Katie yelled, "I won't go without you." She covered her mouth as the air thinned then they both pulled their masks back over their heads.

The couch didn't catch on fire as quickly as the stuffing had. It was smoldering sending smoke upwards in a thick black cloud.

Smoke flooded the plane amplifying the animals incessant yelping and crying.

"I can't breath," Katie complained as she coughed, "I've got to take this mask off."

"No," Jeremy shouted, "Keep it on, it will help filter out the smoke. Katie get away from here. Get back with mom and dad." Jeremy pushed on her shoulder nudging her to get up and move away from him.

"No," she sputtered in between coughs, "no Jeremy, I won't leave you."

The scratching and yelping had stopped. The wind was picking up and the smoldering couch was starting to really burn.

Jeremy stood back up and with a heavy piece of metal he tried slapping the fire out, it didn't work.

"Beer," Katie kept repeating out loud, "Beer."

Jeremy coughed and gasped for air as the oxygen starved room thickened with smoke.

Katie had fallen to the floor and couldn't stop coughing.

Jeremy fell to his knees as the metal rod he had been holding crashed to the floor. He doubled over and fell head first to the ground landing almost on top of Katie.

"Goodbye," Katie he said while gasping for air and going into an uncontrollable coughing spasm, "Goodbye."

The couch was now fully enflamed. The entire insides of the cabin became visible.

"No," Katie cried, "I won't let you die Jeremy." She pulled off her mask and gorilla gloves sat up and looked around the room.

The smoke and fumes immediately attached her throat and burned her eyes. "Beer," she kept repeating in between coughs, "I need beer."

Her knees crunched the glass beneath them as she crawled closer to the bar. Beer cans and bottles were strewn everywhere.

Keeping her eyes closed she felt around for a full can. She opened it and emptied it on top of her head. Then she grabbed two more cans while slowly standing up. She shook both cans as she moved closer to the couch.

Jeremy had stopped coughing and was still. Katie looked down at him as she passed him and said, "Beer, use the beer."

She dropped one can while she vigorously shook the other as she gasped for air.

Her hands were shaking as she popped open the can. Beer foam shot out like a cannon being fired. She aimed it at the flames. When the foam stopped she covered the small opening with her finger and violently shook the can again until fresh foam shot out.

While coughing and gasping for air she staggered around the room picking up cans of soda and beer. She repeatedly shot the liquid into the fire. When the cans stopped foaming she poured what was left inside of them all over her face and hair as she struggled for air.

The flames retreated into bellowing black smoke. The thick cloud spiraled upwards outside into the darkness.

Gusts of winds kept hurling the black cloud downward towards Katie where it swirled around her face sucking away her oxygen.

"Mom," Katie cried as her knees buckled beneath her. Her coughing echoes around the room as she collapsed.

The cabin went silent.

The wind whistled as it shot inside the plane picking up speed and screaming around the cabin tearing up everything in its path.

Metal creaked, groaned and shook as Mother Nature showed her strength. Her wrath fell on silent ears.

Slivers of light pierced the tattered metal and danced into the room.

A thin layer of gray smoke hovered close to the ceiling. The perched couch was slowly rocking and still smothering sending sporadic streams of gray smoke bellowing upwards.

Sections of it looked like burnt marshmallows all black and puffy. Most of it was layered in different depths of gray smoke.

Jeremy and Katie were curled up in a fetal position on the floor directly below the couch.

Katie's hands were cut and bloody. They were tucked underneath her chin close to her face, which was swollen and burned. Her hair was matted and looked like something from a Frankenstein movie.

Jeremy was completely covered in fur. His still body could have been mistaken for a large black furry rug.

Morning came and left without a whisper or movement from inside the wreck.

Gail winds that had ripped through the plane the night before had blown a mountain of snow off of the fuselage.

The sun was bathing on the exposed metal ricocheting off of it like well-polished silver.

"There, I see it, over there," An excited voice shouted, "turn this plane around this instant, I know I saw my plane."

"Yes," Mrs. Thornton a deep masculine voice replied, "We'll go back for a closer look."

Sara Thornton's aged lined face pressed hard against the window as the plane turned.

"Rescue one to Walker Field," a calm voice said, "We have a sighting, circling back for a closer look. We're sixty miles north east of Grand Junction."

"Roger that," a metallic voice replied through a hand held receiver.

"Mrs. Thornton," the pilot said, "I'll do a five mile circle, back over the same area. Let me know when you spot the plane. I'll call back the coordinates to the base camp and they'll send out a chopper."

"Oh no you won't, that's my nephew down there. I want you to land this tin bucket as close as you can to my plane down there, do you understand me?"

"Yes," Mrs. Thornton the pilot replied.

"Hurry up, you idiots haven't been able to find my plane for three days. I've only been in this tin bucket for two hours and I've already found it. You charge me a fortune every time I get inside one of these tin buckets. Oh I'm glad my husband isn't alive to see this."

"There, there it is to the left of those trees straight ahead, yes I'm sure that's my plane. Put this tin bucket down right over there, next to it.

As aunt Sara flung demands at the pilot he calmly logged the coordinates and called them into home base.

"Look, look down there, my plane's on fire," Sara yelled in between babbling on and on about the cost of her airplane, "Can't you do anything right? You went past my plane, I told you to land this plane, can't you hear me?"

"I'm sorry Mrs. Thornton, that's a no go. The area is too heavily wooded to land we'll have to return to base."

Sara verbally lashed out at the pilot as he radioed the base that he was returning.

"Excuse me, Mrs. Thornton," the pilot turned the volume up on the intercom in an attempt to drown out aunt Sara's voice, "A rescue team has already been dispensed and will reach the plane within twenty minutes. We can have a chopper pick you up and bring you back to the crash sight within an hour. Will that work for you, mam?"

Sara's nose was still plastered against the small rectangular window she was sitting next to. Whether she heard the pilot or not was not clear, "Get me a helicopter," she demanded, "and get me one quick. My nephew could be dying down there."

The plane's wing tipped upwards and turned left towards the Walker Field airport.

The skies were clear and dark blue, which painted a colorful backdrop for the thick green forest and white powdered mountains that surrounded the area. Not a cloud was in sight. The wretched winds that had plagued the area over the past few days were gone leaving no visible sign of their existence.

Flocks of birds took to the skies as ardent skiers swarmed the slopes all eager to enjoy the calm picture perfect weather.

"I wanted to thank you Mr. Richfield for hiring me." Rhonda fluffed up his bed pillow as she spoke, "Mary was my best friend here at the hospital. I can't believe that something this horrible could happen to someone that nice."

"Your secretary Tammy just called and said that Mary's plane has been spotted and that a rescue team was transporting her and her family to the Saint Mary's hospital."

"She asked me to check with you first but she thought it would be a good idea if I fly immediately to Grand Junction to help Mary and her family in their recovery. I will call you and keep you informed of their progress. Is this what you would like me to do sir?" Rhonda squeezed Mr. Richfield's right hand as she spoke.

Mr. Richfield's eyes were open without saying a word he slowly shook his head in agreement.

"Thank you sir, thank you very much. I promise I won't let you down."

"That's not fair," Timmy complained, "How come she can go and I can't."

"Timmy," Rhonda explained, "Mary's plane has been located but no one knows how Mary or here family are, I'm a nurse and I can help her. You stay here at the hospital with your parents they need you. When Mary is well enough to travel I'll bring her back here, okay?"

Timmy frowned, "How come everybody here treats me like a little kid. I'm almost nine years old and Mary is my friend, I want to go."

Rhonda walked back over to Mr. Richfield bed. She knew he was still very weak and was not suppose to be talking. His lips were silent his eyes ushered Rhonda towards the door.

"Goodby Timmy," she said as she hurried out the door.

"Gosh dad, I never get to do anything. I'm tired of being in this hospital. When do we get to go home?"

"Hello, excuse me is this Mr. Richfield's room? I'm Cathy the nurse from the agency. Are you Mr. Richfield's son?"

Cathy was a small-framed woman in her early twenties. Her hair was neatly tucked behind a starched white nursing cap. "Can I get either of you gentlemen anything?"

"No," Timmy whimpered, "I'm sick of ice cream and I want to go home."

"Well, maybe I can help you get home." Her soft voice replied.

"What do you mean?" Timmy asked as he lifted his head up to look at Cathy.

"Well, I talked to your doctor a few minutes ago to see how you were doing. He said he was hoping to remove that cast from your legs real soon. Isn't that good news?"

"What does real soon mean?" Timmy asked as a frown returned to his face.

"Well," she continued as she straightened up the books and toys scattered around the room, "If you get lots of rest and eat your vegetables he said in only a couple of days."

"I want to go home now!" Timmy yelled, "and I want to see my friend Mary."

Mr. Richfield's bed was surrounded with hospital equipment that was strewn with tubes and blinking lights.

Timmy was in a separate bed on the other side of the room. It was filled with small plastic toys and a couple of books. Stuffed animals and colorful toys were scattered around the room making it look more like a playroom than a private hospital suite.

Cathy checked all of the equipment by Mr. Richfield then she walked over and sat in a chair next to Timmy's bed. She fingered through the books neatly stacked on a table close to a window.

Timmy pulled his blankets over his head, "I don't want to hear another story and I want Mary to read it to me, I don't like you."

Cathy slowly pulled the covers down off of Timmy's head, "Okay," she said, "I won't read to you and if you tell me where Mary is, I will call her and ask her to come here and read to you."

Timmy was puzzled by Cathy's reply. Didn't she know that Mary had saved his fathers life? Didn't she know that Mary had been in a plane crash? And that pictures of her and her family had been in the newspaper and on the television all week?

Cathy patiently waited for Timmy's reply as he stared into her face. "Can I call her? Do you know her phone number?"

"She's a nurse," Timmy slowly replied, "And she's my friend." He turned his face away from Cathy and tucked it deeply into his pillow.

"If she's a nurse," Cathy said, "Then I'll go find her for you, okay?" Cathy stood up and turned to leave the room.

"No," Timmy cried, "She's...his lip quivered as his eyes filled with tears.

"What is it?" Cathy asked as she sat back down, "Please let me help you Timmy."

"She's on a plane and, and" He repeated as he started balling, "she's lost." His face flooded with tears.

"I'm sorry," Cathy said as she reached down to wipe away his tears, "I don't want you to cry Timmy. Is there anything I can do to help you?"

Cathy's soft caring voice and sincere smile helped calm and dry Timmy's tears as they ran down his face.

"She saved my dad's life and she's a hero and I miss her reading me stories." Timmy choked on his words as the water flowed from his eyes. He was reluctant to pull his head out of his pillow. He didn't want her to see his tears.

Cathy moved her chair closer to his bed and listened to Timmy as he spilled his heart out. He told her about Mary and how she had saved his father's life. He relived every detail that his young mind could remember.

He told her about the car crash that he and his parents had been in. Then he told her how frightened he was until he had met Mary.

Cathy was a captive audience and dried Timmy's eyes whenever he momentary looked up at her. "Wow, that's an incredible story. I can see why you miss Mary."

Cathy wasn't sure what part of Timmy's story was true or which part was make believe. All she knew for sure was that she was a private duty nurse and she was being very well paid to care for Mr. Richfield and his son Timmy and right now Timmy needed a shoulder to cry on.

The afternoon turned into evening, Cathy's compassion and patience paid off Timmy calmed down and finally fell into a deep restful sleep.

"Good morning gentlemen," Cathy said as she pulled the window curtains open. "Is anybody hungry? It's eleven in the morning and its time for both of you sleepy heads to wake up."

Timmy's toys were now neatly stacked in a corner. The balloons that were scattered around the room were now tied down in a bouquet across from the window.

"I thought you two would sleep all day. The nurse that took your vitals at seven this morning said that both of you were dead to the world. I have some very good news for you." Cathy pulled Timmy's blankets off of his head.

She pushed a button on the side of his bed. It made the top half of his bed move upwards, forcing Timmy's body into a sitting position.

"What good news?" Timmy asked as he rubbed his eyes and looked around the room. "Do I get this cast off today?" Timmy was still entombed from the waist down in a thick plaster cast. Moving around was next to impossible in it and over the past two weeks as he gained his strength back it had become almost intolerable. He was constantly scratching and pulling on it as he regained feelings in his legs.

"No," Cathy slowly and casually replied hoping Timmy wouldn't fly into an outrage, "It's better than that."

Timmy frowned at Cathy, then in one fluid motion, picked up his game boy, turned away from her and started playing a game.

"They found Mary and she's alive, isn't that wonderful Timmy? Timmy, can you hear me?"

Mr. Richfield's call button lit up above his bed. Cathy turned towards him and checked the saline solution and medications that were dripping into his arm intravenously.

"Good morning sir," she said as she reached for his left arm to take his pulse. "How are you feeling today Mr. Richfield?" She asked not expecting an answer or reply.

"Mary, you said they found Mary." His eyes opened wide as his weak voice crackled, then they closed and he was silent.

"Why yes," Cathy stuttered as she tried not to seem surprised that Mr. Richfield had spoken. "Yes Mr. Richfield they found the plane late yesterday and." Cathy hesitated, looked around the room then bent down closer to see if Mr. Richfield was awake, "And" She continued, "Mary and her family are all alive and at a hospital in a town called Grand Junction in Colorado.

"Well," Cathy nervously said, "Sir, your blood pressure is back to normal and your temperature has stabilized. Mr. Richfield I'm going to change your linen in a few minutes and sir," she cleared your throat, "Your doctor has taken you off of a liquid diet and put you on a soft diet. I've ordered you real food, soup for lunch."

Mr. Richfield didn't respond to Cathy. He moved his head around, back and forth on his pillow in what looked like an attempt to get more comfortable.

Cathy turned his television on then walked over to Timmy, "Ok young man" she said in an authoritative voice, "Its time for you to get washed up."

Timmy tightened the grip on his game boy as Cathy pulled down his blankets. Timmy she said in a softer voice, "You can play with this later, right now I need to get you clean."

"No" he complained, "I'm not dirty all I do is lay here in bed I'm already clean. Cathy tightened her grip on his game boy while moving her face in front of Timmy's eyes. "You want to be clean when you see Mary, don't you?" she asked with a smile.

"Timmy handed her his game boy while plastering an intense look on his face. "Look," she said, "Your friends are on the television, look up over there on your father's television."

Timmy looked up at the television as Cathy clicked the volume louder. Mr. Richfield's telephone rang at the same time. She handed Timmy the remote control and hurried over to the telephone. "Mr. Richfield's room" she politely said, "Hello." "Hello this is Rhonda, is Mr. Richfield awake?"

"No" Cathy replied, "Can I take a message for him?"

"Yes," Rhonda said, "Would you please tell him that I arrived in Grand Junction safely and that Mary and her family were found alive yesterday. I haven't seen Mary yet but I know that her and her husband are both in the intensive care unit. At this time they are in critical but stable condition. I would like to stay with them until I know that they are out of danger."

"I've called Mr. Richfield's secretary Tammy, she said Mr. Richfield was adamant that I stay with Mary until she recovers. Would you please tell Mr. Richfield that I will stay by Mary's bedside and I will call him with even the slightest change in her condition."

"Hello, did you get all of that?" Rhonda asked as silence filled the phone's receiver. "Hello" she repeated, "Do you understand?"

"Oh," Cathy finally replied, "You must be Mr. Richfield's private nurse."

"Yes" Rhonda replied, "How is Timmy?"

"He's angry and upset about Mary. What would you like me to tell him Rhonda?"

Rhonda hesitated then replied, "Tell Timmy, Mary is alive and in the intensive care unit just like his father was."

"Are you sure? Cathy questioned, "He's very upset and maybe I should tell him that Mary is fine."

"Yes, I'm sure." Rhonda said, "he'll understand. I can be reached at 970-245-0002 I'll call when Mary's condition changes. Oh yes, Mr. Richfield is more lucid in the afternoon, make him sit up and talk to him. Has he talked to you yet?"

"Yes he has," Cathy replied, "But it was only for a moment. He looked so lifeless then out of nowhere he asked me a question, at first he startled me."

"Keep talking to him," Rhonda instructed, "and make him stay awake in the afternoon. He needs as much brain stimulation as we can give him."

"Dad," Timmy screamed before Cathy could hang up the phone, "Wake up, they found Mary, wake up dad." Timmy's voice shook the room, "Dad wake up they found Mary, she's alive, we have to go help her."

Timmy's voice squealed with excitement as his questions flew, where is Grand Junction? How far was it from here? My dad's got lots of planes we can fly there."

Timmy's excitement flooded the room Mr. Richfield must have felt it. His hand reached over and pushed the button to raise his bed into a sitting position. He took a deep breath while opening his eyes as he looked around the room.

"Well hello," Cathy said in a surprised voice, "I'm glad to see your awake Mr. Richfield. Can I get you anything, sir?"

"Mr. Richfield's face was badly bruised and swollen. "Yes young lady," he said, "Get my plane, we're going to Grand Junction Colorado."

Cathy wasn't sure how she should respond to his request. Was her patient delirious? Or was this normal behavior for patients coming out of a comma.

She plastered a nervous smile on her face and excused herself from the room.

"Great," Timmy said, "What plane are we going to take? I like the big red one."

Mr. Richfield turned his head towards Timmy and said, "Good choice son, that's a bell jet. Where's the food around here?" he complained as he looked around the room."

"Here dad I've got some M&M's that Mary snuck in for me, here catch." Timmy threw the bag of M&M's across the room. They landed in Mr. Richfield's lap. The bag split wide open and M&M's flew everywhere.

"Oops, sorry," Timmy said as he watched the display.

"Thank you son, this is just what I needed to get me moving." Mr. Richfield examined a red M&M then slowly put it in his mouth. "Mmm," he said, "I forgot how good these tasted. He grabbed another one, then a fist full.

"Slow down," Timmy complained, "Save some for me, Dad can we really go see Mary?" he asked as he watched his dad inhale M&M's.

"You bet son but we have to keep this our secret."

"What do you mean?" Timmy asked, are we going to be in trouble?"

"No," Mr. Richfield said, "But we can't tell your mother."

"Why not?" Timmy asked, "Can't mom come with us?"

"No," Mr. Richfield replied, "Your mother needs a lot of rest. We'll go pick up Mary and bring her back here before your mother even notices that we're missing."

"Dad," Timmy asked as he lowered the tone in his voice and talked slower, "Are you sure you're all right? I don't want to see the doctors put all of those tubes back into you. I'm strong and I can go get Mary. You stay here with mom and I'll pick up Mary."

"You're a Richfield all right," Mr. Richfield smiled as he threw an M&M at Timmy. Timmy caught it and immediately threw it back at his dad. M&M's started to fly bouncing off of everything in and around the room.

Cathy walked into the cross fire and an M&M almost landed in her open mouth as she watched the fight. "I..I" She stuttered as she took a step backwards hiding behind the door, "I called your doctors they will be here soon."

"I don't want to see a doctor." Mr. Richfield hollered, "I want a plane. Where's my secretary, Tammy?"

"I," Cathy stuttered again, "I don't know sir," Cathy peeked from the safety of the door and looked around to see if it was safe to enter. She composed herself lifting her chin high "I see you gentlemen have already had lunch," she said as she calmly walked around the room picking up M&M's, "I don't think M&M's are what the doctor meant as part of a soft diet Mr. Richfield, please give them to me."

She held out her hand. Mr. Richfield reluctantly opened his fist and dropped the M&M's into Cathy's fingers. "And you," she said as she walked over to Timmy's bed "You don't need any more sugar young man, hand them over."

Timmy glanced over to his father, Mr. Richfield turned his head away in guilt. Timmy slowly dropped a small arsenal of M&M's into Cathy's opened hand.

"Now gentlemen it's bath time," she said as she flushed the M&M's down the toilet, who wants to go first?"

Timmy and his father both tucked their heads deep into their pillows as they turned their heads away from Cathy.

Maybe it was the sugar rush from the candy maybe it was the sponge bath from Cathy but for whatever reason Mr. Richfield was looking and acting like a healed man. His voice was loud and strong. His eyes were clear and bright. The only sign of weakness was his bruised face and the intervenes tubes that were still attached to his left hand.

"Well gentlemen are you ready for lunch?" Cathy asked as she carried trays in from the hallway outside.

"Cathy," Mr. Richfield asked, "Where's the damn doctor and why hasn't my secretary called?"

Cathy acted nervous as Mr. Richfield asked the question. Although she replied quickly and articulately she kept fidgeting with her hands.

Mr. Richfield picked up on it. "You didn't call my secretary did you?" he asked as he raised his bed back into a sitting position.

"I'm sorry," she confessed, "Your doctors orders say no visitors and no phone calls. I called him this morning to see if he would change the orders. He said no, not until he examined you and that he would be here some time this afternoon. I'm sorry sir but I'm your nurse and I cannot change the doctor's orders.

Cathy lowered her eyes away from Mr. Richfield. "Sir," she added, "you have made a remarkable recovery. I'm sure once your doctor examines you he will agree with you. I truly thought he would be here by now." She raised her head back up and forced a smile as she looked into Mr. Richfield's eyes.

Mr. Richfield lifted his right arm up and squeezed Cathy's hand, "Thank you," he said, "Please wake me up when the doctor gets here." He lowered his bed and closed his eyes.

Timmy stopped picking at his sandwich, lowered his own bed back to a sleeping position and also closed his eyes.

Cathy was young and not sure if she had done the right thing. Although she had followed the doctor's orders she was a private duty nurse and she knew that Mr. Richfield was her boss, not the doctor. Mr. Richfield had hired her and he could fire her.

She left the room and called Mr. Richfield's doctor again.

The glare from the sun pierced Mr. Richfield's eyelids. His phone rang at the same time, waking both him and Timmy up.

Cathy was sitting in a small chair next to the window reading a magazine. "I'll get it Mr. Richfield," she said as her hand beat his to the receiver.

"If it's my secretary Tammy I want to talk to her," Mr. Richfield said as he raised his bed back into a sitting position.

"Yes, okay sir, thank you sir," Cathy put the receiver back down. "Well?" Mr. Richfield asked, "Who was it?"

"It was your doctor," Cathy replied, "He was held up in surgery and is on his way over here right now."

"Well, it's about time," Mr. Richfield said as he straightened his sheets tiding up his own bed.

"Can I get you anything?" Cathy asked as she fluffed up his pillow.

"I want some ice cream, chocolate," Timmy said as he sat up and looked at Cathy, "And how about whip cream and caramel sauce?"

"I'll see what I can do," Cathy said as she left the room.

"Dad are you paying the doctors here?"

"Of course I am," Mr. Richfield quickly replied, "Why Timmy?"

"Well, I don't get it. When you pay people at your airport they do what you tell them to, don't they?"

"Yes," Mr. Richfield slowly replied.

"Then why don't the doctors and Cathy do what you ask them to? You're paying them and they're not listening to you, why?"

Mr. Richfield face lit up while he though long and hard on how to answer that question.

"Good afternoon Mr. Richfield, Timmy." A short over weight, balding man wearing old fashion round metal glasses, entered their room.

"Are you my dad's doctor?" Timmy asked as the doctor flipped through a stack of papers he was carrying.

"Yes, young man I am," He politely replied as he pulled his face away from the papers for a split second.

"Then why don't you do what my dad tells you to?" Timmy asked, "He pays you doesn't he?"

"What?" The doctor's eyebrows inched above his eyeglasses and a puzzled look filled his face.

"Mr. Richfield tried to hide a smile that almost touched his ears.

The doctor lowered his eyebrows and cleared his throat as he took a closer look at Mr. Richfield's face and said, "I see you both are feeling a lot better. Now what is this I hear about you wanting to leave the hospital?"

CHAPTER 10

"We have to save Mary," Timmy said, "She needs us."

The doctor pulled a small flashlight out of the pocket of his white lab coat and flashed it in Mr. Richfield's eyes. "Look left, now right, good."

"Head trauma is a very serious matter. I'm very happy with your progress Mr. Richfield but you need at least another week of bed rest. Your cat scans shows multiple tears and those take time to heal. Too much movement could laps you back into a coma."

The doctor took his glasses off, moved away from Mr. Richfield's bed and said, "No you're not going anywhere. I'll order you a light sedative if you need one."

"Dad," Timmy said, "What does he mean? Aren't you his boss? How come he's telling you what to do? Does this mean we can't go see Mary?"

The doctor's eyebrows raised up again as he said, "And I think a sedative might be in order for you too young man."

Mr. Richfield understood what his doctor was telling him but after the doctor ordered the sedative for Timmy he came unglued, "We're going" he said as he kicked his blankets off we'll be back in two days. Mary saved my life and I won't let her down."

"If you get out of bed," The doctor warned, "I'll order bed restraints and I'll sedate you."

"You can't talk to my dad like that," Timmy hollered, "He's paying you and you're not even listening to him."

An arguing match erupted, the doctor's plump cheeks turned red and his calm manner disappeared.

The nurses outside in the hallways quickly filled the doorway and listened. The conversation was anything but ordinary:

"Then I'll buy this bed and I'll buy this hospital." "You can't buy this bed and I'm going to sedate you unless you calm down." My dad is rich and can buy anything he wants."

Cathy stood in the doorway her eyes wide open darting back and forth between Mr. Richfield and his doctor. Neither gave up any ground.

"Excuse Me," she repeated over and over again, "I think I can help." She finally walked over to the left side of Mr. Richfield's bed and threw both of her hands high up in the air while yelling, "Please gentlemen, listen I have a solution."

Her high-pitched voice momentarily caught both men's attention. Both sets of angry eyes fell upon her. Her heart was racing as she took a deep breath and said, "Okay Mr. Richfield your not suppose to be out of bed correct? And doctor you want to make sure Mr. Richfield stays in bed right?"

Both men glanced at each other then back at her, "Then, Mr. Richfield why don't you promise your doctor you won't get out of bed, rent the bed" she said as she smiled. "If it fits in one of your planes then you will be doing what the doctor ordered."

The doctor shook his head totally disagreeing, "I can't allow that."

"Why?" Everybody in and around the room asked, "Why not?" The doctor acted surprised when he noticed the large crowd that had formed around and outside the room.

"I just can't" He stubbornly replied.

"I'll tell you what I'll do" Mr. Richfield said in a calmer voice, "I understand, You just don't want to be liable for me right? No problem, I'll make it easy for you. Someone get me a pen."

A dozen pens clicked on Cathy picked one out and walked it over to Mr. Richfield, He immediately started writing. "There" he said as he handed the doctor the paper while reading it out loud, "I Mr. Richfield will not hold Dr. Skarett liable for any and all medical complications that I might incur away from Saint John's Hospital." "Cathy" he continued, "please get my secretary Tammy on the phone, right now."

Dr. Skarett's pager beeped. He frowned at Mr. Richfield shook his head in disgust and walked out the door.

"Way to go dad," Timmy yelled, "lets get out of here."

The crowd disbursed and phones in the room immediacy started ringing. A parade of people marched in and out of Mr. Richfield's room. Three hours later Mr. Richfield and his son were on a plane headed east.

Cathy and a nurse named Mark were with them. The flight was smooth. Mr. Richfield and Timmy slept as Cathy updated the new nurse Mark on what was happening.

"Mr. Richfield is an amazing man," she said, "He must be a very important rich man. After I called his secretary Tammy a wall of people were crawling all over the hospital in a matter of minutes. I've never seen so many people do so many things so fast. I've never been on a private jet like this before have you Mark?"

"No," Mark replied, "I was shocked when the nurse registry called me and said I would be paid three times my normal wages if I could work within the hour. I dropped what I was doing and drove immediately to the airport. That's all I know."

Tammy, Mr. Richfield's secretary hadn't stopped moving since Mr. Richfield had called her. She carried a cell phone, pager and a walkie-talkie. When she hung one of them up another would start ringing. She remained calm and acted very comfortable in her surroundings.

She was sitting in an overstuffed chair close to the front of the plane her legs were crossed. She was in constant touch with the pilots and occasionally she would walk back to Mark and Cathy and update them on what was going on.

It was daybreak when the plan's wheels touched down at Walker Field in Grand Junction Colorado. Two ambulances and an entourage of vehicles met the plane.

The air was icy cold and the skies were calm and clear.

Mark rode with Mr. Richfield in one of the ambulances. Cathy rode with Timmy in the other.

Mr. Richfield was awake but kept fairly quiet. His secretary was running everything. She constantly glanced back and forth at Mr. Richfield as though reading his eyes and occasionally softly whispered in his ear. Their communication was uncanny.

The ambulances made a loud beeping noise when they arrived at the hospital as they backed up into the emergency room entrance.

Men and women in white uniforms greeted them at the entrance as they helped them inside.

The white walls and polished floors of the hospital were a stark contrast to the ultra modern furnishings of the plane.

"Welcome Mr. Richfield," a tall well dressed man said as he reached down to shake Mr. Richfield's hand. "It's an honor sir our medical staff is at your beckon and call. We've arranged a private room next to the Thompson's children Katie and Jeremy. You'll be on the third floor."

"Thank you," Tammy replied, "Mr. Richfield is looking forward to seeing the Thompson's family as soon as possible."

"Timmy used his elbows to prop himself up in his bed, "We came to wake Mary up. I didn't know she had any kids are they my age?"

"Hi Timmy, how are you?" Rhonda was standing at attention next to the hospital administrator. "I'm not sure how old Mary's children are," She said, "but they're in the room next to yours. If you're not too tired I will take you to their room so you can meet them."

"Lets go," Timmy said, "I'm not tired let's go." Rhonda led the way down the hospital corridors as Mark and Cathy pushed the two hospital beds around.

Timmy was enjoying himself as he pretended his bed was a race car, "Faster, faster" he kept shouting back at Cathy, "Can't you move this bed any faster?"

His excitement and enthusiasm spilled over onto everyone around him who pointed and giggled at him as Mr. Richfield's parade of employees led him around the hospital.

Rhonda stopped at Katie and Jeremy's door. "Thank you Cathy," she said as she bent over for a hug, "thank you for taking such good care of Timmy. I'll introduce him to Mary's children then I'll bring him right back to Mr. Richfield room. I imagine you all could use some rest so I'll wear Timmy out and bring him to your room in a little while."

Cathy joined Mark and helped push Mr. Richfield's bed forward to his room.

Rhonda pushed Jeremy's bed inside Katie and Jeremy's room. They were both sitting up watching television.

"Hi, I'm Timmy," he announced as he entered, "How's Mary?"

Jeremy and Katie both acted surprised "Who are you?" They both asked at the same time. "How do you know our Mom's name?"

"I'm Timmy, your mom saved my dad's life and my dad and I are here to help her."

Katie and Jeremy passed confused looks back and forth to each other. "Sorry Kid" Jeremy finally managed to spit out, "I think you have the wrong room."

Timmy looked around the room and said, "Isn't your mom Mary?"

"Well, yah," Katie slowly replied, "but I don't think you have the right Mary. We were in a plane crash and our mom and dad are down stairs in intensive care."

"I know," Timmy said, "That's why my dad and I are here. We're here to wake her up."

Both Katie and Jeremy's faces were badly swollen and partially bandaged. They both had intervenes tubes attached to their left arms and a thin plastic tube snaked around both of their faces and ended inside their noses. The other end of the tube was attached to the wall.

"What's in your nose?" Timmy asked as Rhonda pushed his bed further inside the room, "Does it hurt?"

"Get out of here," Jeremy yelled in a weak voice, "leave us alone."

"But I'm here to help you," Timmy hung his head down like he had just done something wrong.

"That's no way to treat an eight year old that just flew across the country to help your mom" Rhonda said as she turned Timmy's bed around, "Timmy wanted to meet you. He thought you would be nice like your mother Mary."

"What? I'm sorry" Katie said in a tiny soft voice as she searched Timmy's face, "We don't understand. I mean I don't know you. I mean I live with my mom and I've never met you, have I? How do you know her? And what do you mean you and your dad flew here to help her? I'm tired and what your saying doesn't make any sense to me, please go away."

"Well, well, well," Rhonda said, "Your both finally awake. My name is Rhonda I'm a nurse and I work at the hospital with your mother Mary. Didn't she ever mention my name?"

Katie and Jeremy shared a confused glance and both said, "No."

"Do you mean back home in California?" Jeremy asked as he slowly took a deep breath.

"How about me?" Timmy asked, "Didn't your mom mention me? My name is Timmy."

Confused looks and dozens of questions brought the quiet room to life. Mr Richfield joined in the menagerie.

Timmy relived the experience and told his story about how Mary had woken up his father from a coma.

Rhonda filled in the parts that Timmy had forgotten. Katie and Jeremy listened but were both convinced that their mom Mary couldn't be the same Mary that Timmy and Rhonda were describing.

"I'm sure that couldn't be my mom," Katie said, "She would never threaten anyone with a needle. I just can't believe you."

"Cool, bad, she really did that?" Jeremy was totally enthralled with the story. "I didn't know Mary I mean my mother could be so cool I mean so bad. I always knew there was a reason I liked that woman, yes," he proudly said, "I'm sure of it now."

"Sure about what?" Katie asked.

"About adopting her I'm going to keep her." No one understood what Jeremy had just said but the general consensus around the room was confusion anyway.

Everybody was listening to numerous conversations at the same time and it seemed who ever had the strongest voice got the attention.

Jeremy and Katie threw each other reassuring glances as they described their survival after the crash. The hospital halls quickly filled with curious personal and camera crews.

Flashing lights and camera equipment brought the rooms friendly conversations to an abrupt halt.

Insensitive questions about death and wild dogs sent Jeremy and Katie retreating back under their covers.

"All you people are looking for is a story." Rhonda snapped as she put her left hand over the camera lens. "They're children and they've been through a lot. Get out of here all of you, now."

"Just one more question, please," a rather charismatic voice asked. The room cleared as a tall well groomed gentlemen wearing a three-piece suit entered, "Thank you" he said as he walked into the room, "Who's idea was it to wear the gorilla suits?" he asked. He opened a small pad of paper as he asked the question again, "Please" he said, "I'm from the Los Angeles Times Newspaper. One of you is now a hero and we want to do a cover story on you. Those thick furry suits you were wearing saved your lives and we would like to do a feature story on your survival. We've already talked to your Aunt Sara. She told us you brought the gorilla suits because of her Halloween party, is that true? Did you have them on before the crash?

"That's three questions," Rhonda said as she stepped directly in front of the man blocking Jeremy's bed from his view.

"When may I come back?" The reporter asked as he took a step backwards, "Those gorilla suits saved your entire family's lives."

"You already told us that," Rhonda said as she took a step forward forcing him to back up further.

"Please call me, I promise you we will write the story through your eyes." He handed Rhonda a business card and left the room.

Katie and Jeremy cautiously pulled down their sheets. Their room was silent again. Everybody's eyes focused on Jeremy.

"What? What? Why is everybody looking at me?" he whined, "All I did was put those stupid gorilla suits on everybody so we wouldn't freeze, no big deal."

As it turned out it was a big deal and the word spread like a wild fire. In a matter of hours interviews with aunt Sara were being shown on every prime time television channel.

"Of course I was the one who found the plane. I knew it would be in the Rocky Mountains by Grand Junction. The lucky lady was easy to spot."

"Lucky lady?" the reporter questioned, "Was that the name of the plane that crashed?"

"Yes," she said, "My husband won that plane for me. He told me he was on a business trip and a week later he showed up with this big airplane."

"Wow," The reporter said, "How did he win it?"

"What he told me" she said in almost a crabby voice, "Was that he won it with a pair of sevens. Now don't you tell anybody about this" she said as she put her hand over the camera lens, "That was a long time ago, don't you want to know more about my Halloween parties?"

On a different channel Sara was going on and on about the huge Halloween parties she and her husband had.

"Halloween flight 77" one reporter said, the name stuck. Every newspaper and television station that got their hands on the story called it, "Halloween flight 77."

Camera crews set up camp in the hospital hallways. They hounded Jeremy and Katie every waking minute.

John and Mary's recovery were shadowed in the media frenzy. Mr. Richfield and Timmy had retreated to their room.

Mr. Richfield's secretary assigned the male nurse, Mark to Jeremy and Katie's room.

Rhonda rejoined Mr. Richfield and Timmy.

"Wow," Timmy said, "There's a lot of camera's out there. Dad can you make them go away?"

Mr. Richfield was staring at the ceiling from his bed deep in thought. He knew that Timmy wasn't aloud near the intensive care unit, let alone inside Mary's room.

Rhonda watched Mr. Richfield for a few minutes then said, "I have a plan. I can get Timmy past the media and onto an elevator down to the intensive care unit."

She moved her chair in between Mr. Richfield and Timmy's bed and slowly whispered her plan.

"That's the same thing Mary and I did" Timmy said as he interrupted Rhonda, "I know what to do. Please dad, please can I go?" Timmy's excitement filled the room hearts began pumping faster.

"Are you sure you can do this?" Mr. Richfield asked with a stern look on his face.

"If Mary can do it, I can do it," Rhonda replied as she straightened her nurse's hat. "Give me five minutes then hit the fire alarm."

Their hospital door flew open sending adrenaline shooting through everyone in the room. It was Mr. Richfield's secretary, Tammy.

"Is everything all right Mr. Richfield?" she asked as everyone's eyes fell upon her, "I'm sorry sir I can't get the media to leave. I don't understand their persistence on hammering those children with all of their questions."

"Sir," she added as she closed the door and walked over to Mr. Richfield's bed, "I did talk to the head of security. They're bringing in more personnel and they're going to patrol this hospital floor all night."

Tammy glanced at Rhonda then Timmy and finally her eyes fell on Mr. Richfield, "Are you sure you're all right sir?" she asked again, "something just doesn't seem right in here."

Mr. Richfield smiled and said, "We have a plan Tammy. We're going to shake up this hospital. When did you say that extra security is going to arrive?"

"I'm not positive," Tammy said, "But I imagine within the hour, sir. Would you like me to cancel them?"

"No," Mr. Richfield replied, "I guess now is as good a time as ever."

"To do what?" she asked. "Can I help you, sir?"

Mr. Richfield glanced down to where Rhonda was sitting and asked, Can Tammy help you Rhonda?"

"Well," Rhonda admitted, "I'm not very good with planning things. I'm using the same plan that Timmy and Mary used. If you have a better one I would love to hear it."

Tammy pulled up a chair and sat next to Rhonda as she explained to Tammy how Mary had gotten Timmy into the intensive care unit.

"Hurry up," Timmy complained, "Don't change the plan, I already know that one and I know what to do."

Rhonda and Tammy looked like football players in a huddle as they bent over and threw ideas back and forth at each other.

Mr. Richfield and Timmy watched them as they went into action. "I'll be right back," Rhonda stood up and without looking at anyone she left the room.

Tammy got on her cell phone as she moved her chair into a corner of the room.

A few moments later Rhonda reappeared in the doorway with a modified wheel chair designed for full body casts.

Tammy hung up her phone and said," It will be here in ten minutes." Both women carefully lifted Timmy out of his bed and into the wheel chair.

"Mary wasn't this slow," he complained as both women fastened him in, "lets go."

"I'm sorry Timmy" Rhonda said as she rechecked the safety belts around him, "We're almost ready."

A few minutes later a small package was delivered to the room. Tammy signed for it then opened the box. She pulled out a curly gray wig and a thick gray mustache.

"Who's wearing that?" Timmy asked as Tammy fluffed up the wig.

"You are," Mr. Richfield chuckled, "You're an old man. Son we all figured you would have a much better chance of getting into the intensive care unit by pretending to be Mary's father.

"This is a dumb plan," Timmy complained, "I liked Mary's plan, this plan is stupid." Timmy fussed and complained as Rhonda put the wig and mustache on him.

"Give me five minutes," Rhonda said as she left the room with Timmy.

"Timmy, you have to be real quiet. Look away from people and keep your head down, do you understand?"

"I don't like this wig." Timmy complained, "It itches, why can't we use Mary's plan?"

"No," Rhonda immediately replied in a stern voice, "And I'm not going to take you downstairs to the intensive care unit unless you listen to me and you must do what I tell you to, okay?"

"Okay," Timmy grumbled, "But I'm taking this stupid wig off as soon as we wake Mary up."

Rhonda carefully guided the awkward wheel chair past the mountain of camera equipment and electrical cords.

Like Mary's plan she covered Timmy's head with a hospital blanket and quietly slipped him onto the elevator. Unlike Mary's plan the elevator filled up with people. Most of them were holding styrofoam coffee cups and caring camera equipment.

"Hello," one reporter said, "Do you work in this hospital?" Everyone in the elevator started laughing everyone except Rhonda and Timmy.

"That was the stupidest question I have ever heard." Another reporter chuckled. "You see a nurse inside the hospital with a patient in a wheel chair and you ask her if she works here. The elevator filled with laughter once again.

Rhonda plastered a nervous smile on her face as her heart pounded out of her chest. Please Timmy she thought, please don't say a word.

The elevator chimed and the door opened on the first floor. Rhonda and Timmy exited first and headed down the hall towards the intensive care unit.

The herd of reporters headed in the opposite direction towards the front entrance of the hospital. They were still chuckling and teasing the reporter that had asked Rhonda a question.

"Can I talk now?" Timmy softly whispered as he poked his gray head out from under the blanket.

"Shh, shh" Rhonda whispered back, "We'll wait here until Tammy sets off the alarm. "Please stay quiet and don't show your face to anyone especially one of those reporters. I was sure they knew that something was wrong. I am so nervous. "Why do all of those people have to be here?"

"Shh, shh" Timmy teased, "You're louder than me. Aren't you going to hide me in the bathroom like Mary did?"

"No," Rhonda replied, "I didn't know Mary hid you in the bathroom."

As Timmy explained what Mary had done a loud overhead speaker interrupted him.

"Please move to your closest exit sign this is not a drill", it kept repeating in a calm but very loud voice that was followed by a mind splitting high pitched beeping noise.

"It's not loud enough," Timmy complained, "Mary's noise was much louder, are you sure Tammy pulled the right switch?"

A wall of hospital personal walked past Timmy and Rhonda all heading towards the hospital's front door. "Can I help you?" every other one of them asked as they reached out for the wheel chair.

This was not part of Rhonda's plan. "Find a bathroom," Timmy shouted, "hurry up."

"No thank you," Rhonda kept nervously replying, "we forgot his purse, I mean his wallet." She pushed the wheel chair forward and turned it into the first open door quickly closing it behind her.

Timmy pulled the blanket off of his head, "This isn't how Mary did it, and you're too slow." he complained, "Hurry up Rhonda, I have to go to the bathroom."

Rhonda took a deep breath, covered Timmy's head back up and causually poked her head out the door. The hallways were deserted. She pushed the wheel chair down the hall and hurried towards the intensive care unit.

CHAPTER 11

Timmy poked his head out from under his blanket as Rhonda pasted the first intensive care room, it was empty so was the next room. Oh my God Rhonda thought, they moved the patients outside because of the fire, now what do I do?

"Excuse Me," a loud voice said, "You're going the wrong way. You need to turn around and head down the hall toward the front exit. Do you need any help?"

The voice was directly behind Rhonda. She froze while thinking what to do then she slowly turned the wheel chair around to head towards the exit.

"No," Timmy yelled, "keep going."

"Rhonda?" A surprised voice squealed.

"Janet?" Rhonda said as her voice shook with fear.

"What are you doing here?" They asked each other, at the same time.

Rhonda was visibly nervous. Janet had fired her less than a week ago and she could tell that something wasn't right.

"Is something wrong?" Janet asked as she studied Rhonda's face and stepped closer to the wheel chair.

"No," Rhonda quickly replied, as she calmed her racing heart, "Nothing is wrong."

"This wouldn't be Timmy by any chance, would it?" Janet asked as she studied the blanket on Timmy's head.

"No, no Janet, I'm helping Mary's father. He lives here in Colorado and he has hired me to help him with Mary and her family." Rhonda was a bad liar and Janet knew something wasn't right. Without permission she ripped off the blanket from Timmy's head exposing his gray hair and mustache.

As though on cue Timmy immediately tucked his chin deeply into his chest and coughed.

Janet's face filled with surprise as her eyes focused on Timmy's gray hair, "I'm so sorry," she said, "Please forgive me sir I thought you were someone else."

Rhonda covered Timmy's head back up while throwing Janet a dirty look. "He's tired and the light hurts his eyes." She calmly said as her heart raced. "Janet" she asked in an authoritative voice, "I promised Mary's father I would bring him to see his daughter today even if only for a few moments. Do you know where Mary's room is? I was told that she was in the intensive care unit."

"They are here," Janet replied as she lowered her face in embarrassment. Mary is in the room at the end of this hall. I flew in yesterday and visited with her this morning, I was hoping I could wake her up. Well," she sighed, "it didn't work. I hope her father can help her." Janet turned and followed the rest of the crowd outside.

"Whew," Rhonda sighed, "I was sure we were going to be busted that time."

Timmy pulled the blankets off of his head, "That was really funny. That lady thought I was an old man. I'm going to wear this wig all the time, this is fun."

"Thank you Timmy," Rhonda said as her voice shook, "I was so scared, when my x-boss Janet pulled that blanket off of you, I thought I was going to die."

"You're sure not like Mary," Timmy said as he turned his head around and looked up at Rhonda, "But that was a lot of fun, can we do that again? Was that women really your old boss?"

Before Rhonda could answer Timmy the alarms stopped ringing, a second later Timmy spotted Mary. "Over there" he shouted, "There she is, Rhonda Mary's over there."

The nurses' station was still deserted. Rhonda glanced behind her, the wall of people that had left the hospital a few minutes ago, were all on their way back inside.

Her heart jumped into her throat, "We've got to hurry," she said as she opened Mary's door, "The nurses are almost back here already, keep quiet Timmy."

"Why?" Timmy asked, "I fooled one nurse why can't I fool them all?" Rhonda pushed his wheel chair as close to the head of the bed as she could.

"Excuse me," A nurse said, as she appeared in the doorway, "No visitors are allowed in here today you will have to come back tomorrow."

Timmy lowered his head and looked away from the nurse. Rhonda smiled at her then put her index finger over her lips and said, "Shh, shh this is Mary's father he is saying goodbye to his only daughter. We'll be out of here in just a few more minutes, this is so sad." Rhonda's face filled with sadness as she pretended to cry.

The nurse glanced around the room as she said, "I guess it can't hurt her, Mary's a real trooper. I don't know how she survived in that plane as long as she did with all of her broken ribs and a punctured lung. Have you watched the news about her family and their accident?"

"No," Rhonda calmly replied, "I didn't know she had children." The nurse lowered her head as though in grief and said, "It's a shame, Mary has a wonderful family and they must love her very much. Her children have been on the television all day today, they really tried hard to save her life." As the nurse walked away she mumbled in a sad voice, "How come things like this always happen to families that really love each other? It's so sad."

Rhonda held her breath, closed the door and turned away to face Timmy, as his eyes met hers they both exploded with laughter.

"I didn't know she had children" Timmy mimicked as he threw his arms up while laughing. That was great Rhonda, I think that nurse believed you."

"I can't believe I said that," Rhonda giggled, "I've never been a good liar." She straightened her spine and stood tall in between laughing fits that made her keel over.

"You're really funny," Timmy roared. His face filled with laughter and his gray mustache fell off making the situation even funnier."

"Mary wake up" he chuckled, "It's me, Timmy." He picked up the mustache and held it close to Mary's eyes. It fell from his hands as he giggled and landed on Mary's face just below her nose, it fit her face perfectly. His giggling turned into an uncontrollable outburst of laughter. He pointed at the mustache for Rhonda to see she started giggling. Timmy's laughter was contagious and Rhonda's eyes filled with water as she tried to control herself.

"Wake up Mary," Rhonda said as she composed herself, "Timmy's got a present for you."

Timmy squeezed Mary's right hand and started tapping on it, "You've got to wake up." He chuckled, "You've got to see your new mustache."

Their laughter circled around the room then shot out into the hallways through the large glass windows that surrounded three sides of the room.

The door opened and the doorway filled with curious bystanders. Laughing wasn't something that occurred often around here, especially this kind of an outburst. The laughter was contagious and everyone within an ear's reach jointed in as they watched Timmy point to the mustache on Mary's face.

"Who are you?" an older woman in a white uniform asked as she pushed her way to the front of the crowd, "What are you doing in this room?"

Timmy twisted his neck around and joked, "I'm Mary's father, can't you tell by my gray hair?"

"Call security," the older woman shouted, as she turned and exited the room, "Don't just stand there, didn't anyone hear me? Call security, that's a boy in there." The tone in her voice sent a shockwave to the crowd they stopped laughing.

"Please wake up," Rhonda pleated as her face filled with worry," Please Mary wake up they've called security."

"I don't care," Timmy said in an angry voice, "I'm not leaving until Mary wakes up. Come on Mary" he kept repeating, "wake up, I'm here to rescue you, you've got to wake up just like my dad did."

A minute later two thick men in dark green suits appeared in the doorway. "This patient is really ill" one of them said in a calm voice as he glanced around the room, "You'll have to leave right now."

"I'm not leaving until Mary wakes up," Timmy yelled as he pulled off his wig. "Look Mary," he cried as he tapped her hand harder, "It's me, Timmy your friend, remember me?"

"I'm a nurse," Rhonda nervously said as one of the security guards took a step inside the room. "Timmy is Mary's son, please let him stay, he's trying to wake his mother up."

"Nice try," the other guard said in a deep voice as he took a step closer towards Timmy, "Lady, I don't know who you are or who this boy is but I know that this kid isn't Mary's son. Her children are upstairs, I just checked on them. This is a hospital and you both have to leave right now."

"Wait," Rhonda shouted stopping both guards in their tracks, "Don't come any closer." She thought about what Mary had done to hold off the guards from Timmy's father. Her eyes searched the room looking for a weapon. The guard's eyes followed hers. There were no needles or anything in the room that remotely resembled a weapon. Her heart pounded out of her chest as panic filled her mind.

She stepped backwards retreating to the left side of Mary's bed and grabbed the liquid packet and intervenes tubes that were attached by needles to Mary's arms. "Leave us now," she shouted, "Or I'll, I'll turn these intervenes drips wide open."

Timmy looked up at Rhonda with a puzzled look on his face. "What will that do?" he asked. "That's not what Mary did to my dad, won't that hurt her?"

"Now!" a guard shouted as he flew towards Rhonda. "Got him," The other guard announced as he pulled Timmy's wheel chair away from Mary's bed.

Rhonda fell to the floor as Timmy screamed and bit the other guard. "Ouch!" The guard yelled, "This kid bit me."

Timmy latched back on to Mary's motionless hand and held on to it with all of his strength, "Wake up Mary, I need you, please wake up."

Mary's fingers began to move and squeezed back on Timmy's tiny hand, "Look" he cried, "Mary's waking up."

Rhonda was petrified and as the guard picked her up off of the ground she fainted. "What did you do to her?" The other guard asked as he watched Rhonda slip back down to the ground like a wet noodle. "What are you doing to her?"

"I don't know," The confused guard replied as he reached for a tighter grip on her body as she slipped back down to the floor, "I swear, I didn't do anything to her." he shouted.

"You hurt my friend," Timmy yelled, "Dad," he screamed as loud as he could, "Help, these guys are hurting Rhonda."

The commotion quickly brought an audience back to the room, this time a camera crew was with them.

"Get that camera out of here," a nurse yelled. "Look over there." another loud voice yelled. "I don't believe it," another person commented. "Get that on film" a reporter shouted.

Mary's fingers were now all moving first on her right hand then on her left hand. The odd thing about it was that John her husband was in the next room and his fingers started moving exactly at the same time that Mary's had. Mary raised her right wrist John raised his.

"This is weird," A spectator said, "How come that guy in the room next door is moving his hands and body at the same time that that women in that other room is moving hers? Is this supposed to be happening?"

Everyone's head turned to look at John, and then they turned back towards Mary's room. The halls filled as John and Mary simultaneously regained consciousness.

Rhonda and Timmy were not aware of what everyone else was watching. They didn't even know that John was in the room next door. They were both overwhelmed and relieved that everyone's eyes were focused on Mary, not on them.

Mary took a deep breath as she tossed her neck around on her pillow. Her eyes opened, a second later John's eyes opened. Monitors in both of their rooms buzzed and beeped as they both started breathing on their own.

The halls filled with clapping and cheering that echoed around the hospital like wild fire.

Timmy's tiny voice was drowned out as he said, "I love you Mary can you hear me?"

Mary turned her head toward his voice as a nurse pulled a tube from her mouth. She blinked her eyes a few times and a smile lit up on her battered swollen face. Her lips moved but no words could be heard, tears filled her eyes.

"All right," Timmy shouted, "Your going to be all right, just like my dad." His eyes closed as he yawned and said, "Can we go home now Mary? I'm really tired, I've got some new books to read."

I recognized Timmy's voice but I didn't know who he was. I knew I was in a hospital but none of my surroundings looked familiar. My head was throbbing and I was dizzy with clouded thoughts.

"Hello Mary," a soft voice said drawing my eyes upwards it was Rhonda. Rhonda I thought what is she doing here? Our boss Janet fired her, what was she doing back here at the hospital?

I opened my eyes wider and blinked a few times hoping it would help clear the dizziness that was swirling around inside my head. I focused on Rhonda face as a flash of bright lights blinded me confusing me even more. I shut my eyes and retreated to my pillow.

"Stop it," Rhonda shouted, "Get those camera's out of here, somebody get those camera's out of here."

Rhonda's voice was comforting. I remembered how she made me laugh at work. Work? Wait a minute was I at work? Why was I in bed? I blinked a few more time while opening my eyes wide once again.

I was in a room surrounded by strangers it sent my heart racing. Timmy squeezed my hand drawing my face away from the wall of people. "It's okay Mary, I'll have my dad get rid of these people."

Why were these people here? Why was I here? I studied Timmy's face searching for answers.

Rhonda kneeled down close to Timmy and said, "Welcome back Mary. We weren't sure that you were going to make it. How are you feeling?"

I heard what Rhonda had just said to me but it didn't make any since. Why would she be asking how I was feeling? I took a deep breath hoping it would clear my mind as I tried to sit up. My ribcage exploded in pain. Frightening memories of the plane crash flooded my mind sending me retreating to the warmth of my pillow.

John, where was John? That's it! I thought, I'm in a hospital, I'm alive but where is John? Where is Katie? With each question I asked myself my heart pounded faster. As it raced I remembered more and more about the plane crash. None of thoughts made me feel any better they all frightened me.

"It's okay, it's okay Mary, everything is all right." Rhonda turned my head towards her face. "Mary" she said, "You've been through a lot but the worst is over you're going to make it. Do you understand me?"

I couldn't stop thinking about John. Where was he? My skin was puffy and it felt like it had been stretched like a blown up balloon and my lips felt like they were twisted inside out. I knew I was moving them as I spoke to Rhonda but I couldn't feel them.

"Don't talk," Rhonda said as she stroked my cheeks, "You've been through a lot and you need to get some rest. Timmy and I will take care of the rest of your family for you Mary."

I could hear Rhonda but I hadn't heard her mention the name, John. My family? Did she mean Katie my daughter? I opened my eyes as wide as they would let me and I squeezed her hand as I studied her face.

"Look," she said, "look up there." Where? I thought as my eyes glimpsed around the room.

"Up there," she said as she pointed to the television set attached to the wall a few feet away from me.

"Quiet everyone," Rhonda said, "somebody turn up the television, Mary still isn't sure where she's at."

The faces that surrounded me all turned their heads towards the television, my eyes followed there's. The room got real quiet as the television blared.

"How does it feel to be a real hero?" a woman reporter asked. "I'm not a hero," Jeremy replied as the camera's closed in on his face.

Wait a minute? Was I seeing things? That was Jeremy. What was he doing on the television?

Rhonda must have sensed my confusion. She squeezed my hand while she glanced and smiled at me then she looked back up at the television.

I blinked my eyes over and over again hoping my thoughts would make more sense to me. My eyes followed Rhonda's back to the television.

"And how about you young lady," the same reporter asked, "Do you think your brother is a hero? Was that gorilla suit comfortable?"

It was Katie, my heart skipped a beat, she was alive, and she was on the television.

The camera focused back on the reporter. What had Katie just said? I didn't hear her but whatever she had just said brought instantaneous laughter to the crowd in my room.

Katie and Jeremy were alive I felt a little relieved. Where was John? A nagging voice inside of my head wouldn't go away. It kept asking the same question over and over again. Was John alive? I felt like crying but I didn't.

I looked back up and glued my eyes to the television and listened closely hoping they would say something about John.

"These modest teenagers saved their parents lives," The reporter continued,"And they both say it was no big deal. I can only hope that my children could be as brave as these two children were, if something like this happened to my family. Their parents must be very proud of them right now. This is Rachael Long for KSTP news with an updated report on the crash of Halloween Flight 77."

Had I just heard the reporter correctly? She said Jeremy and Katie saved us, and she said parents, not just mom. A huge weight lifted off of my heart as I realized that John was alive, but where was he?

Everyone around me started clapping as the television was turned off. Faces and eyes I had never seen before flooded me with kind words and warm thoughts. It was overwhelming I retreated back to the safety of my pillow.

"I know what's wrong," Timmy, blurted out, "Mary wants to see her husband, like when my mom and dad got hurt and wanted to see each other. Where is he?"

I wanted to sit up and kiss Timmy. I remembered how frightened he was when he was all alone in the hospital after his car accident. I remember visiting his room every free minute I had and when I couldn't find a book to read to him I remember the fun stories I told him about John.

John, the name flew around the room. "John is right next door," a familiar voice said.

I turned toward the voice it was Janet my boss. At first the sight of her frightened me. What was she doing here? Or was I in her hospital? My thoughts were tiring me.

"Hi Mary," she said as I closed my eyes, "Your husband is in the room right next door. I have some good news for you he just regained consciousness and wants to see you. How is your headache?"

I opened my eyes and forced air deep inside my chest, it hurt but it felt good. John was alive and close by, my kids were alive, my family had survived.

I had so many things to tell everyone. I wanted to hug Katie I wanted to thank Jeremy I wanted to kiss John. I missed my family.

I closed my eyes and thought about how wonderful it was to have such a special family.

About the Author

Debbie Madison is a self-made woman who by her 21st birthday had built her first house and a successful accounting practice.

Her zest and optimistic outlook on life are the building blocks that propel her ambition and passionate nature.

HALLOWEEN FLIGHT 77 is her first fiction novel in a line of stories that she paraphrases as: Quick Reads. Fast paced, real life drama with extensive dialogue and explosive characters that immediately pull you in and keep your attention.

www.ingramcontent.com/pod-product-compliance
Lightning Source LLC
Chambersburg PA
CBHW030341290526
45785CB00004B/1558